# The American Revolution
## —— ON ——
# LONG ISLAND

# *The* American Revolution

## — ON —

# LONG ISLAND

Dr. Joanne S. Grasso

THE
History
PRESS

Published by The History Press
Charleston, SC
www.historypress.net

*Front cover*: "Battle of Long Island," by Alonzo Chappell, 1858.
*Courtesy of the Brooklyn Historical Society.*

*Back cover, top*: "Map of the Progress of His Majesty's Armies in New York During the
Late Campaign." *Courtesy of the Geography and Map Division, Library of Congress. Bottom*:
"Washington's Retreat at Long Island." *Courtesy of the Digital Collections,
New York Public Library.*

First published 2016

Manufactured in the United States

ISBN 978.1.46711.828.6

Library of Congress Control Number: 2016936011

*This book is dedicated to the American Revolutionary generation of Patriots*
*and*
*to my mother's heritage from that generation.*

# Contents

# Acknowledgements

There are many people for me to thank for help in the research for this book. Because it is my first book, I felt even more of a need to seek out those people, organizations, libraries and historical societies that could offer direction and guidance.

Natalie Naylor at the Long Island Studies Institute in Hofstra University in Hempstead, New York, was particularly helpful and encouraging in obtaining information both in the institute and elsewhere. And the research librarians at the institute were very accommodating during my many visits there, looking through the vertical files and making copies of information.

Thomas Fleming, a renowned American Revolution author, and his wife, Alice, gave direction for photos, illustrations and permissions. He was a mentor to me of sorts and a personal associate through our mutual American Revolution Round Table of New York City.

Professor Georgina Martorella, chair of Reference Services and the Collection Department at Hofstra University Axinn Library, is thanked for her direction in obtaining books and research material on the Continental Congress.

Thanks to Jean Amaral, Assistant Professor of the Kurt R. Schmeller Library at Queensborough Community College, for her help and encouragement in publishing and photos for books. She gave a great seminar in which I gathered quite a lot of introductory information on contracts as well.

The Queens Historical Society gave wonderful direction in looking for historical societies. Although it told me that the society did not have

American Revolutionary items, it gave me solid leads on which historical societies might have them.

The Connecticut Historical Society in Hartford was also very helpful in research direction.

I used the United States Merchant Marine Academy (USMMA) library for copies of "Letters of Delegates to Congress: 1774–1789." Although the Government Documents section of that library is not as extensive as those at other libraries, it has some excellent selections for American government research.

And the gold mine of historic books and Long Island documents at the Manhasset Public Library in Manhasset, New York, is second to none. This library was particularly gracious in allowing me to look extensively at its private collection and make copies when necessary.

The Brooklyn Historical Society was a wealth of information about that area and about Long Island during the American Revolution. It has archives with manuscripts and papers, as well as books, maps and other information related to this period of history. And what better place to study the American Revolution than in proximity to the area where the Battle of Long Island took place!

Polly Guerin, a fellow American Revolution Round Table Board of Governors member, has been both a great help and a mentor to me as I began working on this book and limped along at times in need of information. As an author for this same publisher, her guidance has been invaluable.

The Queens Library in Flushing was a great resource, and the help of the librarians was much appreciated.

I was able to solicit solid information from the archivist, Angelo Vigorito, of the General Society of Mechanics and Tradesmen.

The Library of Congress has been of immense help in securing images and information for images.

Thank you to the Huntington Town Historian's Office for all of the material its staff scanned for me and the time they allowed me in their files.

The Missouri Tourism Office and the Missouri History Museum in St. Louis were gracious in allowing me an image from their collection.

The Society for the Preservation of Long Island Antiquities deserves praise for its help.

The New York Historical Society also deserves thanks for its information.

The Suffolk County Historical Society allowed me a lot of time in its files for research and was of great help in securing further information.

# Acknowledgements

I cannot say enough about the East Hampton Library, Long Island Collection, particularly librarian and archivist Andrea Meyer, who continually provided excellent resource information, images e-mailed and general direction all throughout the writing process.

Fred Blumlein, a longtime friend and trustee of the Cow Neck Peninsula Historical Society who is also a retired adjunct professor of Pratt, was very generous in providing me access to images of the Sands-Willet House, the Cow Neck area and a story about a woman from the Sands-Willet House.

The Three-Village Historic Society was very nice in sending me images needed and providing resources for that area.

The Wisser Library at New York Institute of Technology, particularly Danielle Apfelbaum, was very gracious and particularly helpful in giving me information to work on the practical aspects of this book.

I would also like to thank all of the local historic sites and historic societies that preserve American Revolutionary history on Long Island.

Finally, I would like to thank the editors and staff at The History Press for facilitating my first book. This book truly was a work of love and oftentimes required more work than even I originally thought. My passion for studying the American Revolutionary generation was greatly helped by this publisher.

# Introduction

In researching and studying the American Revolution, one cannot help but be overwhelmed by the suffering of a generation of people, particularly in a contained area like Long Island, which was under occupation.

There is solemnness to the study of the American Revolution on Long Island. From the horror of the British prison ships in Wallabout Bay in Brooklyn to the courage of the boat raids on the North and South Forks on the eastern end, the American Revolution created the infrastructure of a very difficult history. Though often covered over with paved roads and modern buildings today, this history is as real and alive as it was in 1776.

Enclosed in these chapters are photos of historic homes and buildings, people who lived through the American Revolutionary era and sign markers where historic sites were located and battles took place. Many of these homes with original walls have been added onto or refurbished in some way. Some, like Raynham Hall in Oyster Bay, have a few original furnishings from the Townsend family and remembrances of the son there who was intricately involved in the spy ring on Long Island.

The intention of this book is to keep American Revolutionary history alive by encouraging people to go out and experience it in an era when technology instead simply brings history to a person. My overall purpose is to educate the public about American Revolutionary history on Long Island and to urge people to go out and see the historic sites and markers. There are many more people, historic sites, events and sign markers that were not included

The Old House, Cutchogue. *Author photo.*

because of space but have equal importance to the history presented in this book. Part of the wonderful layers of American history on Long Island is the American Revolution. It is one of the layers that will be brought to life here as a "composite" history set in themes. Long Island has had many layers of history, from the Paleo-Indians to the colonials, right up to the post–World War II boom and modern suburban sprawl, as is evidenced in *Newsday's Long Island: Our Story.* However, the presentation of the American Revolution on Long Island has been only part of most histories.

The American Revolution inspires generations even today. In the period of history when it took place, it was regarded with the "deepest veneration." The people of that generation were honored, but as generations passed, the memory of that generation passed as well, along with the "feeling for those times." When a generation such as the Revolutionary generation lives in perilous times and puts its life on the line, it achieves fame at least for a few generations afterward.[1]

Long Island in the American Revolution deserves a larger notation in American history. Most accounts of the American Revolution on Long Island seem to end at the Battle of Long Island, but the war—and indeed, the Revolution—was much greater. Predominant thought is that the door closed on Long Island after the Battle of Long Island in Brooklyn Heights,

A black-and-white graphic of Long Island. *Courtesy of Natalie Naylor and Hofstra Long Island Studies.*

and nothing happened afterward. In fact, when perusing history books and looking for "Long Island" in the indexes, usually just the Battle of Long Island is mentioned, with no other notation about the occupation. But that is not the whole story. It is here that British prison ships took many lives. It is here that George Washington relied on the accounts of spies to aid his army and where he came in 1790, the year after his inauguration, to thank those same spies. Many of the books, booklets, pamphlets and websites used will attest to the fact that Long Island history continued after the Battle of Long Island and did not just fall into oblivion until the end of the war.

What effect did all of the trials, economics acts and the Battle of Long Island in Brooklyn Heights have on the occupation of Long Island? This answer and others will be revealed here. A short compilation of documents is included in the Appendix to help answer these questions.

There is something to be said for being able to indulge in something you love, and for me that is the American Revolution. There is a great reason for my wanting to write this book. A generation of Patriots, including my ancestors of that generation, suffered physically, psychologically and financially in order to bring about this Revolution. And then there are those people from that generation who died and those who were left with nothing at the end of the war. Their stories need to be retold; the generation needs to be remembered and brought to life again for a new generation of history lovers. The Revolutionary generation should be thanked again and again by us, their posterity, for their sacrifices.

## Chapter 1

# The Struggle for Independence on Long Island

There were no divided loyalties or "fence-sitters" on Long Island before, during or after the American Revolutionary War. Nor was there a complacency of loyalty, due to commercial reward, to the winning side that affected other parts of the colonies-turned-states; rather, there was always a sense of urgency that undergirded the infrastructure of life on Long Island at that time. Even daily routines were affected by the overpowering and often ravaging presence of British and Hessian troops.

The last twelve years prior to the Lexington and Concord battle in the Boston area of Massachusetts, which heralded the start of the war on April 19, 1775, would prove to not only set the former British colonies on a conflagration course but also ensure seven long years of British occupation on Long Island starting at the end of August 1776.

Long Island had a myriad of cultures in the 1770s, with three distinct counties—Kings, Queens and Suffolk—which today encompass two of the five New York City boroughs in the counties of Brooklyn and Queens and the counties of Nassau and Suffolk as well. From one end of Long Island to another, the land mass was 118 miles long and 23 miles wide then and now.

The colonies-turned-states lived under the Articles of Confederation (see Appendix), an amazing document for all thirteen states to agree to. Although life on Long Island was a microcosm of the larger picture of the American Revolution in New York, Long Island was unique in its response to the occupation of the British. "While the island would be occupied by the

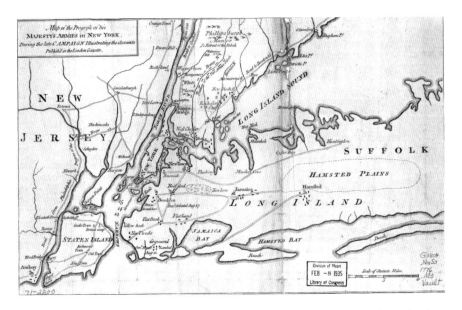

"Map of the Progress of His Majesty's Armies in New York During the Late Campaign."
*Courtesy of the Geography and Map Division, Library of Congress.*

British for the rest of the war [after the Battle of Long Island], its people would not be passive."[2]

The question is, was Long Island just an extension of the greater war in the North and South, replicating itself in battles, skirmishes and confrontations of politics, or was it its own political and military entity, formed out of the physical isolation of a moat with access only by water?

In *The Battle for New York*, author Barnet Schecter puts forth a scenario in which Long Island had a "unique topography" that was crucial to the "strategy and tactics of both sides [of the war]"[3]

The politics of Long Island created a deep division, which eventually created a physical split of the land as well:

*The Loyalist-Patriot split within Queens County's population impacted its local government. Colonial Queens was made up of the towns of Jamaica, Flushing, Newtown, Oyster Bay, and Hempstead. The last two towns today are part of the present-day Nassau County. In September 1775 the largely Loyalist town of Hempstead refused to elect delegates to the Patriot Provincial Congress, whereupon the Patriot communities of Great Neck, Manhasset, and Roslyn seceded and formed the town of North Hempstead, a separation ratified by the legislature on 16 April 1784.*[4]

18

The struggle on Long Island was so strong that it was not only a physical separation but also a division in the hearts and minds of the inhabitants:

> *Long Island was the home of farmers, engaged in raising produce of some sort or other, and the presence of armed men on either side, the constant condition of excitement, the surprise parties that performed their daring feats for the Continentals, the constant surveillance of the military forces of the Crown as the years of occupation passed on and the military necessities of the situation caused the grip, as it were, of the Crown on the island to remain unrelaxed, if not to become tighter as the prospects of Continental success became clearer and more pronounced.*[5]

Even though Long Island was not the physically accessible land that it would be decades later as America acquired more states, the division in the loyalties of the people to the Crown or the Patriot cause created a physical division that, during post–Battle of Long Island occupation, would contribute to whaleboat raids on Long Island by Long Island refugees who fled to Connecticut.

Many items were destroyed by Patriots to prevent usage by Loyalists who stayed on Long Island and who enjoyed the protection and companionship of the British troops.[6] And then there were others, like the Culper Spy Ring, who stayed on Long Island but "fought" covertly. Long Island was a mass of different loyalties. To say that there was a middle section of undecided people on Long Island who did not care who won would be inaccurate. Occupation forced the people to either stand with the Patriot cause or with the Loyalists and the Crown.

The very essence of revolution was brewing long before the first shots were fired at Lexington and Concord. Stirrings of political liberty were in the philosophies of the seventeenth and eighteenth centuries of Europe and its colonies. Britain and France saw policies that pitted the rights of the people against the rights of the monarchy. Hereditary rights created a long-standing obligation of the people to obey laws, however arbitrary, that would stifle their existence.

The last twelve years prior to Lexington and Concord showed that there was an economic and political logic that inevitably led to the Revolutionary War. The colonists were ready to take leadership of this portion of the continent that had come under their own oversight, with the Atlantic Ocean on one side and the Appalachian Mountains on the other side. The question of which empire had the right to this land was initially settled as a result of the

French and Indian War, also called the Seven Years' War, which culminated in 1763. But for some, the rights were not as clear whether England or the colonists were due ownership of this land. "The danger to America it was believed was in fact only the small, immediately visible part of the greater whole whose ultimate manifestation would be the destruction of the English Constitution, with all the rights and privileges embedded in it."[7]

However, for Long Island, the question of rights was clear for both sides in the struggle. The Declaration of Rights of 1774 (see Appendix), written in Huntington, was clear in its patriotic loyalties.

# The Acts

The seeds of independence were sown in the colonists from the moment they set foot in this New World. The causes were always political and social, whether or not they were economically based. These were seeds that seemed to be sown into the ground of the colonies long before the American Revolution. The Sugar and Molasses Act of 1733 led to trade difficulty and selfishness on the part of Great Britain, which kept the colonies in a dependent trade position. The luxury of sugar and molasses production took up land, while the staples of life were neglected.[8]

There was the Proclamation Line of 1763, the Currency Act of 1764 and one of the most offensive acts to the colonists: the Stamp Act of 1765. This act "required that all official and public documents, such as wills, deeds, mortgages, notes, newspapers, pamphlets, should be written on stamped paper or provided with stamps sold by the distributing agents of the British government."[9] "The British Parliament had, by the Stamp Act, undoubtedly usurped the most precious right of the colonists, that of voting their own taxes."[10] And the Stamp Act Congress was held in New York.

There were other economic and political acts after the Stamp Act. The Townshend Acts of 1767 "levied heavy duties on ream glass, lead, paper, and painter's colors imported into the colonies."[11] There was resistance to paying these duties and opposition to bringing in any British goods into the colonies. Prominent individuals like George Washington and Patrick Henry openly resisted the taxes in their colonial assemblies. Even though one colony—Massachusetts, or more specifically, Boston—was the prime target of the British, all of the colonies supported one another in their resistance.

And therein lay the real problem with colonial rule at the time. The colonies had learned to be self-sufficient, and by the time of the Revolutionary War on April 19, 1775, and the Declaration of Independence on July 4, 1776, they were ready to govern themselves.

After the Boston Massacre in March 1770, the Tea Tax by Lord North and the British Parliament meant to salvage the British East India Company by passing along the tax to the colonists and not forcing the company to pay the duties. Every schoolchild should know the backlash for this tax was the Boston Tea Party, which happened not just in Boston but also in other areas.

By 1774, the Coercive Acts—or Intolerable Acts, as the colonists called them—had been set in motion as a result of the Boston Tea Party. Town meetings "were forbidden to convene without the governor's permission, [and] public buildings designated by the governor were to be used as barracks for the troops"[12] (a precursor to the horrors of occupation on Long Island). As a result of the Intolerable Acts and a culmination of years of economic and political hardship, the colonists moved quickly in their committees to have the First Continental Congress in Philadelphia.

The original colonists who had come here for religious freedom and the increasing numbers of colonists arriving from England contributed to a divided political atmosphere that would engulf Long Island as well.[13]

A new nation had already emerged here long before the American Revolution started. This nation saw the British laws differently. This was a gradual but firm change.[14] And the people of Long Island embraced this change; by the time of the Revolution, they stood firmly as either Patriots or Loyalists.

This Revolution would be no easy task for Long Islanders. The split, which culminated in the Towns of Hempstead and North Hempstead, would prove to be an example of the severe divisions in all thirteen colonies-turned-states. For the people of North Hempstead, where the Patriots split from the southern area of the Town of South Hempstead, there was great significance. The British government, which had long been arbitrary in its application of policies, was temporarily in control of Long Island after the Battle of Long Island but with a strong base of opposition both from within and from outside its borders. The hardships and sufferings of the Town of North Hempstead would be most grievously felt.

There were deep divisions in these towns. "Anguish and dissension," along with "bitterness and resentment," described the Town of Hempstead.[15]

Patriots and Loyalists alike vied for control of this part of Long Island. The heightened tensions were only magnified after the Battle of Long

Island, when an assured Patriot zeal gave way to occupation by Loyalist and British troops alike. This period has been called by one historian "the first declaration of independence in America."[16] "The military importance of Long Island at the time of the Revolution resulted from its proximity to New York City. Whoever controlled New York would have to control Long Island as well, or he would be in constant danger of attack from forces which could collect and organize on the Island."[17]

## Chapter 2
# Loyalist Sympathies Divide an Island

As independence loomed, Loyalists—those people who were loyal to King George III, Parliament and Britain—were also called Tories, a more political affiliation. The Patriots preferred to call them the latter. The British failed to significantly use their loyal citizens in the colonies, even though they were in the majority. On Long Island, they could have been an even greater ally for them. There were Loyalist associations and corps of Loyalists everywhere; the Boston area was the first to have a concentration of them, at least until after the British departed. In areas where British troops were fewer than Loyalist numbers, the Loyalists were used in a more efficient manner.[18]

On Long Island, after the largest landing of British troops anywhere on Staten Island and their transition to Long Island, the Loyalists were needed less as security. However, with the major British win at Brooklyn, there was a great amount of prestige given to the Loyalists.[19]

Many different Loyalist regiments were raised, including the very structured oversight of a Paymaster, a Muster Master and an Inspector General. The units formed after Long Island and New York fell to the British contained most of the Loyalists in the colonies.[20]

In Huntington, the Patriots knew who was a Loyalist. The Patriots tried a guerrilla warfare of sorts to harass the British soldiers as they came and went in areas like Lloyd's Neck. As the soldiers were returning to their encampment at night, a rope was stretched across the road to pull the riders off their horses. The soldiers were then placed as prisoners on a whaleboat

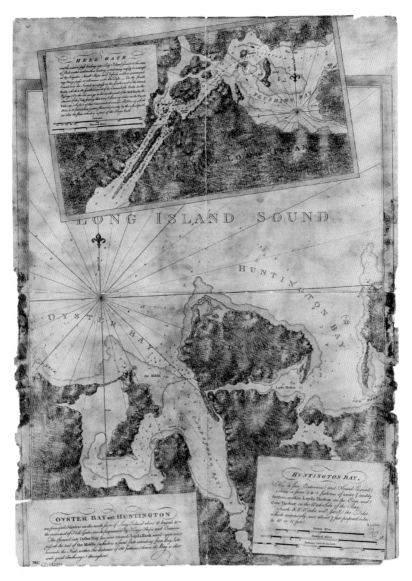

Map of Oyster Bay and Huntington Bay. *Courtesy of the Geography and Map Division, Library of Congress.*

and brought over to the Continental army in Connecticut. Additionally, the Patriots would ambush soldiers traveling alone or with only a few others, at which time the soldiers might be beaten or even killed.[21]

The economic and political acts of 1763–75 divided the loyalties of citizens into the two groups of Patriots, or Whigs, and Loyalists, or Tories.

Often, these loyalties were a matter of heart because of a strong connection to the colonies and independence or to Britain and British heritage.

New York was the colony that contributed more to British military power than any other colony. New York also had more Loyalist claimants at the end of the war to recover taken property. On Long Island, there was a strong presence of Loyalist forces, including the Queens Rangers stationed in Oyster Bay.[22] Additionally, Suffolk County had several Loyalist units, including the Kings American Dragoons, the Loyal Queen Light Dragoons, the Loyal Suffolk County Militia and De Lancey's Brigade. De Lancey's Brigade was one of the more well known of the Loyalist units, originally supposed to be solely on Long Island serving in the Smithtown area, but it was also used elsewhere.[23]

The militias of Long Island from Kings, Queens and Suffolk Counties were revamped in 1776 to become a better fighting force against the British. Complete rolls of the individuals who participated are written in documents, with leadership in charge of each county. Many prominent individuals of the counties put forth to the New York Provincial Congress, along with pounds of powder contributed by their areas of the county. Minute Men companies were also put together.[24]

Feelings against Loyalists ran high on Long Island. They were an entrenched group with their own underground committees of correspondence, which were a "secret means of communicating." Loyalists were particularly numerous in Kings and Queens Counties.[25]

The Loyalists were at once both sought after by the British and at the same time reluctantly used or not used at all.[26] Their "loyalties" to the British Crown often determined where they lived as well. In an area of Queens County, now part of present-day Nassau County, a split was created in September 1775 between Hempstead and North Hempstead and ratified in April 1784.[27] This separation of territory according to loyalty seemed in sharp contrast to New York City, where "there had been more Tories than Whigs among the city's large property holders at the beginning of the conflict."[28] In fact, "two thirds of the City of New York and suburbs belong to Tories."[29]

*Even supposing the majority of islanders were enthusiastic Tories, which they certainly were not, they could hardly have been more severely used had they been pronounced Whigs. They were in fact neither regarded as Kings Men or Continentals; without the need of careful watching by the party in power. Their loyalty to Britain was praised in dispatches to London, but a sharp watch was kept by the military leaders on all their doings.*[30]

On Long Island, one of the homes that was occupied by Loyalists was Rock Hall in Lawrence. Rock Hall, which was in the Town of Hempstead, was pillaged by Patriot forces. Until Long Island was occupied by British and supported by Loyalists, Loyalist homes were in danger of invasion by Patriots.[31] Once occupation happened after the Battle of Long Island in August 1776, Loyalists were safe, at least for the next seven years.

Up until 1775, when word went out about the first Provincial Congress, the twelve years leading up to the Revolutionary War had produced the Town of Hempstead as solidly loyal to the Crown. This area was fairly entrenched with large, wealthy landowners, church officials and peace-loving Quakers.[32]

The North Shore, as one present-day designated area of Long Island is called, was and is more like New England, with its culture and history intact, than other areas of Long Island. In 1775, the commercial interests of this northern area of the Town of Hempstead felt a kinship with the Revolutionary interests of New England.

Connecticut, where Loyalists fled, was easy to get to from Long Island, particularly the North Shore, especially the areas that extended out into the Long Island Sound and created a smaller body of water. Eaton's Neck, opposite Stamford, was one such area.[33] As hostilities grew, not only Loyalists fled to Connecticut, but Patriots did as well. There were whaleboat raids from Connecticut aimed at the Loyalists who stayed on Long Island. These attacks included theft, physical violence and vandalism. The whaleboat raids, conducted by Patriots from Connecticut, kidnapped, ransacked homes and traded prisoners with the British.[34] These local attacks were conducted by both Loyalists who were on Long Island and Patriots who came down to Long Island. The attacks served to help unsettle Long Island for seven years after the Battle of Long Island. Often a place lacking support by government on either side, British soldiers on Long Island pillaged and abused even the Loyalists, most of the time without punishment.

In Queens County, the Loyalists were disarmed as early as the later part of 1775. In January 1776, Washington sent General Charles Lee to take action against the Tories on Long Island, "and his treatment was very severe."[35]

After the Battle of Long Island, the Loyalists were protected for the most part, but they had a tenuous position with the British soldiers nonetheless. Not entirely accepted as pure British prior to the Revolutionary War, they were used by the British during the war in Loyalist military units, as spies and as vandals against the covert Patriots still living on Long Island after the Battle of Long Island.

There were also criminal elements in the Tory regiments who enlisted for their own monetary gain. But because of the need for these enlistees, punishments for crimes were often minimal, or they were overlooked entirely.[36]

There were many active recruiters of Tory regiments. One of the more legendary ones was Edmund Fanning, whose father-in-law was Governor Tryon. He was well connected, well educated and a sharp supporter of the Loyalists. His service as a military leader was marked by cruelty and bloodshed, which became worse as he put together a regiment called the Associate Refugees, or Kings American Regiment. Like many Loyalists, he would have been deeply affected by a loss of position, property and connection had the Patriots won the war.[37]

Another Tory recruiter was Major Robert Rogers. He was called a "soldier of fortune" and was a spy of whom even Washington was aware. While under arrest and parole, he put together a regiment called the Queens Rangers, which many Loyalists from Long Island joined after the Battle of Long Island. The Queens Rangers served in Oyster Bay after the campaign around Harlem.[38]

Loyalties often divided families and even households. Tories were in Kings County, and many active royalist elements were in Queens County. Participation in the newly formed Provincial Congress was often the dividing line of loyalties, whether or not delegates were sent. The decision not to send delegates and to consider more extreme measures, such as poisoning George Washington in April 1776, was blamed partly on the prosperity of the bucolic life (of the Loyalists) and their pursuits.[39]

*Chapter 3*

# Kings County and the
# Battle for Brooklyn

There were many Tories on Long Island, but fighting for independence was not a priority. In 1775, the New York Committee of Correspondence called for each county to elect delegates. The towns in Kings County chose their delegates, and at a meeting, all of the delegates but Flatlands named five representatives to go to New York to join the Continental Congress, which reconvened in Philadelphia in May.[40]

In a September 2, 1776 letter to John Hancock, George Washington wrote of the tumult and despair caused by the Battle of Long Island but also of the necessity of continuing forward in the struggle for liberty:

> *Our situation is truly distressing—The check our detachment sustained on the 27th has dispirited too great a proportion of our troops and filled their minds with apprehension and despair—…I am persuaded and as full convinced, as I am of any one fact that has happened, that our Liberties must of necessity be greatly hazarded.*[41]

The biggest mistake the British made was in underestimating the colonists' ability to carry out an extended war. General James Grant, a member of the British Parliament, had declared on April 19, 1775, just before the beginning of the war at Lexington and Concord, "that the Americans would not fight, and that he would undertake to march from one end of the continent to the other with 5,000 men."[42] However, the battle for Long Island had established a format for the rest of the

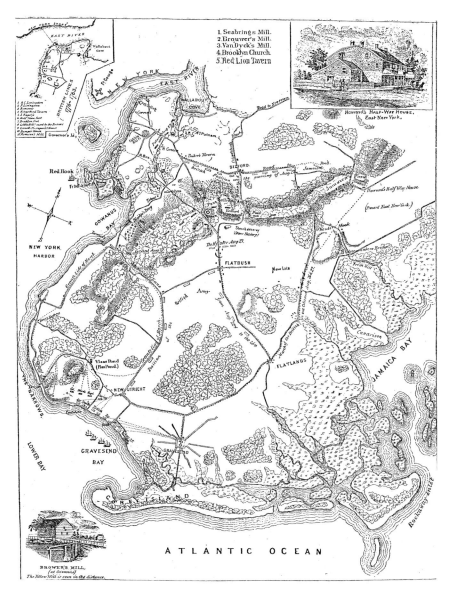

Battle of Long Island. *Courtesy of Prints and Photographs, Library of Congress.*

war. The British would often succeed in their first maneuvers only to be "outfoxed sooner or later by patriot countermeasures that prevented an overwhelming British victory."[43]

But this was still only the beginning of the war, and this battle was to prove both crucial and providential. In July 1776, the British landed the largest forces they ever had on Staten Island with the intention of ending the rebellion in the colonies.

The Battle of Long Island started well before its actual beginning on August 27, 1776. Since loyalties were split, Patriot committees tried to persuade citizens to support independence, and both Loyalists and Patriots took sides on the Declaration of Independence. The fleet that the British assembled on Staten Island between June and August, prior to the battle, was the largest fleet they would assemble at any time. An army of thirty-two thousand well-trained British and Hessian soldiers assembled to combat the militias and still new Continental army.[44]

The Battle of Long Island required months of long preparation for both sides of the war. On August 22, 1776, fifteen thousand British and their forty pieces of artillery that had been on Staten Island were brought over to Brooklyn. Their landing at Gravesend Bay was without incident. The Americans had already fortified their positions in and around New Utrecht, Gravesend, Flatlands and Flatbush. There were four passes to the Patriot fortifications. Even though George Washington was in charge, the change in Patriot commanders under him in the area led to some instability over the course of the battle. Greene became ill and was replaced by Sullivan and then by Putnam. The battle preliminaries began with skirmishes in the early morning hours of August 27, but the main battle waited until the late evening hours, closer to 9:00 p.m. One of the four passes, Jamaica Pass, was easiest for the British to access. Sullivan was taken prisoner, as were many of his men. Stirling and his men fought valiantly, particularly at the old stone building, which was called the Cortelyou House and was near Gowanus. Some of Stirling's men drowned trying to escape across the creek, and the rest were captured along with their leader.[45]

The British, under Lord "Howe[,] embarked 20,000 men and 40 pieces of artillery in small boats at Staten Island and landed them on the beach of Gravesend Bay. It was eight miles from the Brooklyn lines, and Washington was in no position to prevent or hinder the movement."[46] Information could be difficult to discern. The Tory farmers contributed geographical information of Washington's position, and Washington was uncertain whether the real landing of Howe's troops would be on Manhattan. Washington used his own judgment and every day sent reinforcement troops to Long Island. He was concerned about the "lack of vigilance and discipline of the troops" and sent a letter to Putnam admonishing him to "form proper lines of defence around your encampment and works on the most advantageous ground."[47]

The British plan was well thought out, and with the advantage of an overwhelming force, they would succeed, but not before Washington's troops gave a good showing. Some of the events included the positioning of the troops through the Jamaica Pass; Sullivan's moving to and defending the Flatbush pass; Stirling's inflicting a massive amount of death on the enemy; the ten thousand Guards, Highlanders, Light Dragoons and infantry who reached the Jamaica Road about five miles from the American line; the Americans, without cavalry, who had to use small bands of officers with their own horses; the escape and scattering of Sullivan's men; the Bedford Pass, which proved treacherous for Sullivan in particular; Stirling's escape through the swamp; and the exhaustion of the British troops.[48]

*More than two hundred and fifty brave fellows, most of them of Smallwood's regiment, perished in this deadly struggle, within sight of the lines of Brooklyn. That part of the Delaware troops who had first crossed the creek and swamp, made good their retreat to the lines with a trifling loss, and entered the camp covered with mud and drenched with water, but bringing with them twenty-three prisoners, and their standard tattered by grape-shot.[49]*

After Washington and his men retreated, Washington had a conference of his generals in the home of Philip Livingston, later known as the Teunis Joralemon House, in Brooklyn. At this conference, it was decided not to fortify the works even though Glover, Mercer and others had arrived. In fact, Glover would secure all kinds of boats, and he and his men ferried Washington's men across the East River to New York City on August 29; this process took until the morning of August 30 to complete.[50]

The retreat was called by Fiske "one of the most brilliant incidents of Washington's career. Had Washington allowed himself to be cooped up on the Brooklyn Heights, he would have been forced to surrender; and whatever was left of the war would have been a game played without queen, rook or bishop."[51]

According to Major Bourmeister of the Hessian forces, "This day we took eleven hundred prisoners and on the 28th picked up another 426. The total of their killed and wounded is not yet known, since they lie scattered in the woods, where many of the wounded will perish miserably."[52]

The assemblage of troops was a show of force to fully and finally push the colonists into submission. This was to be an assault of major proportions by the British. Washington knew this as well. Most of his forces would also be stationed in this region of Brooklyn Heights. But by August 29 and 30, Washington and his men had been outmaneuvered and outflanked by Howe and his men. The human cost was 1,500 of American forces and 400 British and Hessians.[53]

"The night after the battle was a weary yet almost sleepless one to the Americans. Fatigued, dispirited, and many of them sick and wounded, yet they were, for the most part, without tent or shelter. To Washington it was a night of anxious vigil."[54]

George Washington had a providential retreat from Brooklyn Heights. While campfires were kept burning, John Glover, a Marblehead, Massachusetts fisherman, and his men ferried with boats and oars Washington's men off Brooklyn Heights over to lower New York City under the cover of darkness and with a covering of thick fog. Washington would be in one of the last boats.

*Colonel Glover's Massachusetts regiment, were composed chiefly of Marblehead fishermen and sailors hardy, adroit, and weather-proof; trimly clad in blue jackets and trousers. The detachment numbered, in the whole, about thirteen hundred men, all fresh and full of spirits. Every eye brightened as they marched briskly along the line with alert step and cheery aspect.*[55]

This trial would begin occupation of Long Island. For the next seven years of the war, Long Island would endure occupation by the British, with their Hessian allies, and Loyalist treachery that would end only when many Patriots fled to Connecticut and other areas or when the war ended and occupation ceased in December 1783.

Sir William Howe's report from the Camp at Newtown, Long Island, on September 3, 1776, stated, "On the 22nd of last month, in the morning, the British, disembarked near Utrecht on Long Island without opposition."[56] The entrenched positions of the British in the pass from Flatbush to Brooklyn continued from the village and from the ferry at the Narrows through Utrecht and Gravesend to the village of Flatland.[57] The days progressed slowly from August 26 to August 27 as more land was seized, reaching all the way to Jamaica by August 26. By August 27, Light Infantry and Light Dragoons were firmly opposing the Patriots, who were vacating the heights.[58]

Washington and his Council of War met and decided to withdraw forces from this area across from his New York City headquarters; called "Four Chimneys," that was the site of planned withdrawal of troops.

By August 29, the Patriots were able to evacuate under covert maneuvers, led by General Washington:

*After Washington had compelled the British to evacuate Boston, the three major generals Howe, Clinton and Burgoyne assumed the conduct of the war against the rebellious colonies in May 1776. Washington tried to defend New York, but Howe's superior force of veterans drove Washington's militia from Brooklyn Heights, Long Island and compelled him to retreat step by step through the city of New York and up the Hudson, then across the river into New Jersey, and then across the state of New Jersey to a safe position on the western banks of the Delaware River.*[59]

*General Howe thought that he had Washington in a trap, but found himself mistaken, and was greatly mortified when he found that the whole army had escaped.*[60]

As soon as the battle was over and the evacuation of Long Island by the Continental army and militia was completed, the British lost no time in occupying the area. There was a lack of coordination among the British commanders but a readiness to use some of the "unspiked" guns from Fort Stirling on the escaping Patriots—to no avail. The British were not ready to pursue. They would have needed hours to coordinate efforts, and there was also the possibility that they would destroy part of New York City in their pursuit. The British did not wish to destroy it but to occupy it. So the strategy was to stretch out their forces overlooking Manhattan and Harlem Heights.

Washington needed information from the British lines. He wanted "harassing parties" to go over to Long Island to obtain information. He wanted to defend New York City and felt that he could if "the men would do their duty," but he also felt this would not happen. He was counseled not to hold on to New York but to abandon it. Some of Washington's leaders were actually in favor of destroying New York City so the British could not occupy it. Nathanael Greene and John Jay were among those who supported this option.[61]

The day after the Battle of Long Island, the British brought their ships around New York City with the intention of surrounding and capturing the Continental army. Washington chose Nathan Hale to acquire the information he needed in a covert manner. John Glover's men ferried Washington's men across the Hudson and then their supplies up the Hudson River to Dobbs Ferry. Regiments of Americans took up positions to stop the British from landing at Kips Bay.[62]

The twelfth of September was decided as evacuation day, along with moving the sick and supplies. On the fourteenth, Washington established his headquarters at the Morris Mansion, and by the fifteenth, the British had occupied Manhattan as well. The British left five thousand soldiers to occupy

A view of New York, Governors Island and the River from Long Island. *Courtesy of Prints and Photographs, Library of Congress.*

Long Island. Long Island was considered by the Continental Congress to be only marginally supportive of independence because of the overwhelming numbers of Tories in Kings and Queens Counties, excluding what would become Patriot North Hempstead. Suffolk had a predominant number of Patriots. There had been a "call" from the Continental Congress in 1775 and early 1776 for military support from Long Island. "The returns are exceedingly meagre but enough remains to show that the spirit of liberty dwelt among the people."[63]

Kings, Queens and Suffolk Counties all sent militias with officer leadership, although there is not a complete record of exactly how or whether they participated in the Battle of Long Island. Suffolk County sent Colonel Josiah Smith's regiment, and Colonel Floyd "headed a detachment of militia that was suddenly called to repel a boat invasion from a British ship at the outset of the war; but the Suffolk patriots were ready to do their duty when called upon and gave many evidences of that."[64]

## PRISON SHIPS

One of the cruelest parts of the Revolutionary War was the imprisonment of Patriots on the infamous prison ships, which were mostly docked off

Brooklyn. The most infamous of these was the *Jersey*. These ships, and in particular the *Jersey*, were British ships that were stripped of all the riggings and masts and turned into floating prisons. The *Jersey* was moored off Brooklyn with 1,200 prisoners stuffed into its rotting hull. A cruel story tells of the tossing of a bag of apples into the mass of prisoners just to see them scramble for the fruit.[65] Disease, starvation and depression were all rampant in these inhumane prisons. People were generally left to die; in fact, 11,000 deaths were credited to these hulks. The bodies were carted off the ships and buried in shallow graves along the shore.[66] For years, bones surfaced on the shore. Years later, an obelisk monument, now in Fort Greene Park, Brooklyn, was constructed, and the gathered bones were placed in its base.

The prisoners on these ships were considered traitors by the British, but their treatment and punishment was unbefitting of animals much less human beings. It was noted that their treatment would have been "like a band of pirates waiting to die, which would have been better than to have been sent to the prison ships."[67]

The prison ships were condemned vessels of war, totally unsuitable as places of confinement. The *Jersey* was old and condemned at the age of forty-four years.[68] Food on board the prison ships was putrid, stale and generally damaged, with the British government being charged for the best provisions while providing the worst. There was hope for relief in a couple of ways. There were hospital ships that had slightly better conditions and also exchanges of prisoners. Hope might also come in the form of visits from family, money secretly sewn into clothing to purchase freedom or oversight by Hessians instead of the British. Although different accounts vary about the treatment and length of time most prisoners spent on these ships, capture and imprisonment were oftentimes fatal.[69] As of September 15, 1776, the British occupied Long Island. Prisoners were housed not only on the prison ships but also in buildings in New York City. The Sugar House and the Old City Hall were two of these buildings. "The prisoners taken August 27 were also put in the churches of Flatbush and N. Utrecht but they were neglected and allowed to wallow in their own filth with infected air."[70]

## PEACE SOUGHT

The Battle of Long Island produced an entirely different atmosphere in Brooklyn for the citizens before and after. Prior to the battle, Loyalists were subject to poor treatment by the Patriots. After the battle, when the British occupied Long Island, any Patriot who was still in residence was subject to oaths of loyalty, theft of possessions, theft of livestock and occupation of their homes by troops. Loyalists, believing themselves devoid of ill treatment by the British, oftentimes were the objects of derision. Such was the case with the theft of horses and cattle while they were either being ridden or used.[71]

Brooklyn did create attempts to make peace with the king's commissioners in a letter dated November 1776 in which it was asked for a return of Kings County to "His Majesty's protection and peace."[72] The letter was signed by approximately four hundred men, many of whom left legacies through their descendants and their property. A further letter dated December 4, 1776, from the Provincial Congress, the County Committee and the Committees of the different Kings County townships acknowledged the authority of the king and their own dissolution as a sign of submissiveness to the Crown.[73]

*Chapter 4*
# The People of Queens Resist on Both Sides

Prior to and during the Revolutionary War, Queens County was the epitome of divided loyalties, both ideologically and physically. There was "daily friction between Whig and Tory, which added to the complications and discomfort of war."[74]

Pre-Revolutionary Queens County included the Towns of Jamaica, Flushing, Newtown, Oyster Bay and Hempstead. Hempstead was mainly Loyalist and had adamantly refused to be included in the delegation to the Patriot Provincial Congress. Thereby, the communities of Great Neck, Manhasset and Roslyn separated from the Town of Hempstead in September 1775 and formed the Town of North Hempstead, officially ratified after the Revolutionary War on April 16, 1784.[75] These communities are still part of the Town of North Hempstead today.

The Towns of Hempstead and North Hempstead were so disparate in their political attachments that it was suggested that the North Shore area of Queens County was very close to the New England area and was therefore influenced exceedingly by the "Revolutionary spirit so rampant in Connecticut."[76] Patriotic separation was inevitable.

The people of Queens were not unacquainted with the difficulty of colonial rule but chose practicality over ideals. Landholdings, religion, politically established officials and the interests of a rural population all contributed to a desire for the Tory part of Queens to stay loyal to Britain.[77] The Loyalists even presented an address to then Governor Tryon affirming their loyalty: "We entreat your Excellency to present our

Allen House, Great Neck. *Courtesy of the Great Neck Library.*

Map of Brooklyn and Queens. *Courtesy of Digital Collections, New York Public Library.*

petition in behalf of the well-effected county of Queens, that it may again, in the bosom of peace, enjoy the royal favor, under your Excellency's paternal care and attention."[78]

The internal politics of the area of North Hempstead were so contentious that after a committee of Benjamin Sands, Adrian Onderdonk and John Farmer was formed, Loyalists were arrested. Occupation would bring relief for Loyalists from strife with Patriots, but only until the war ended.[79]

Queens County was a focal point of troops stationed on Long Island. The British Regular Army, Royal Welsh Fusiliers, Hessian mercenaries and American Tories all billeted here. The treatment of the colonists by each of these different occupying regiments was not always polite or fair. The Tory regiments had a lot of cash-for-enlistment criminals who committed unpunished crimes against the citizens.[80] The Hessians were generally easier to deal with and more compassionate in their oversight of prisoners on the ships in Wallabout Bay.

As part of the upkeep of provincial and Crown records, there are detailed records of the proceedings of the time leading up to the split between North and South Hempstead and the occupation years after the Battle of Long Island. Votes of separation were taken at Jamaica, Newtown, Flushing and Oyster Bay. Congress had to consider the matter of Queens in its overall picture of New York. Congress's authority over Queens County was in question, and the resistance of the Loyalists to sending deputies became evident when Congress had to send resolutions to oversee the entirety of Queens:

> *Whereas, a majority of the inhabitants of Queens County in the colony of New York, being incapable of resolving to live and die freemen, and being more disposed to quit their liberties then part with the little proportion of their property that may be necessary to defend them…yet it be reasonable that those who refuse to defend their country should be excluded from its protection and prevented from doing injury.*[81]

The Battle of Long Island in August 1776 would be the dividing timeline of ill treatment of Loyalists. Prior to the battle, they were hunted by the Patriots and taken prisoner. After the battle, the Queens Loyalists were allies, more or less, of the British. In a letter from General Charles Lee on March 5, 1776, he states that there must be open knowledge of whether certain people are enemies of the cause of liberty. He writes, "You are, therefore to secure their persons, and send them up without loss of time, as irreclaimable enemies to their country, to close custody in Connecticut."[82] Some of the most patriotic areas of Great Neck and Cow Neck prevented Loyalists from moving into them, as they had become "a nest to those noxious vermin."[83] The Loyalists, prior to the Battle of Long Island, were menaced as early as late 1775. By early 1776, George Washington had sent General Charles Lee to mete out treatment against the Tories, and that treatment was harsh. Their possessions and livestock were seized, and the items and animals were sold at a greatly reduced price to pay fines against them.[84]

The State of New York also seized the property of anyone who was not amenable to the American cause. There were laws passed in 1778, 1779 and again in 1784 to support this end. The laws even continued up until the War of 1812. After the Revolutionary War, the Commissioners of Forfeitures, who represented Queens, Suffolk and Richmond and handled the forfeiter estates of Loyalists, paid to the New York State treasurer certificates in the amount of £502,709. These compensations and claims were done in general after the war and were not done in areas that were occupied during the war.[85]

But Queens County was different after the Battle of Long Island. Under British occupation, an order was issued by Viscount Howe that read, "No flags of truce are in the future to pass between Connecticut and occupied Long Island, without special license of the General commanding his Majesty's forces, nor any correspondence by letter or otherwise permitted. Flags of truce are in future to be consigned to New York [City] only."[86]

Parts of Queens suffered greatly both in the divisiveness within the county between Patriots and Loyalists and from ill treatment by the British and Hessian soldiers. In Newtown in March 1776, Patriots "secured the whole body of Tories on Long Island in order to put the city of New York and its environs in a state of defence."[87] As a Whig stronghold, even flags of the monarchy and displays of loyalty to the Crown were openly combatted.[88]

After the Battle of Long Island on August 27 and the chaos of August 28, "Newtown was now open to the enemy, and many of the Whig families, alarmed at their defenceless condition, fled in the utmost confusion."[89]

The Tories could be a vicious lot in openly accusing their neighbors of being part of the independence cause. Connecticut became a haven for fleeing Patriots. Many left from the wharfs out in Suffolk County with families, bags and other possessions in the hope of finding a safe existence in a neighboring Patriot state. "Two days after the Battle [of Long Island,] the Convention recommended to the inhabitants of Long Island to remove as many of their women, children, and slaves, and as much of their grain, to the main, as they can."[90] Guildford, Saybrook and Lyme, Connecticut, were some of the towns that aided the fleeing refugees, as requested by different

Towns of Suffolk County, Long Island. Oftentimes, though, with the added financial pressure brought on by scores of refugees, Connecticut Patriots' patience would run out, and the refugees had to return to Long Island to take their chances at life under British occupation.

## Flushing

Flushing was occupied by the British within forty-eight hours after the Patriots lost the Battle of Long Island. Any survivors were hunted by the British, beginning the torment that would characterize the next seven years of occupation.[91]

Flushing was an area where the British occupied homes. A British officer, a prominent Loyalist and a local justice of the peace would stop at homes and demand to use them for billeting soldiers. Even though the Quakers were neutral, both sides took advantage of them. "Flushing furnished comfortable quarters for both officers and men. The favorite toast was: 'A long and moderate war.'"[92] It had been a bastion of loyalty to the Crown prior to occupation.

By 1775, Patriots were struggling to secure support for their cause due to certain attachments—such as to royal governors who lived there and were married to the wealthy, leading families of the area. There were also numerous Quakers in residence who opposed war, Dutchmen who were more interested in their farms than war and Episcopalians who felt loyalty to their connection to a religion of British descent.[93] Well-known and ordinary citizens alike were rounded up to face the horrors of British prisons ships or forced to face a life of exile.

Francis Lewis's home was in Whitestone. Francis Lewis was a signer of the Declaration of Independence. The British, under "Col Birtch, surrounded the [Lewis] house, then seized Mrs. Lewis and destroyed the books, papers and furniture that were in the house. She was imprisoned for several months and would have been without the common necessaries of life, but for the faithful attendance of negro servants who followed their mistress, and ministered to her wants."[94] She was held for several months on a prison ship without a change of clothes or a bed. The depredation of her stay on the ship so diminished her health that she died shortly after being released, which itself occurred only because of the intervention of George Washington, "who ordered the wives of two British officials imprisoned in

Philadelphia until Mrs. Lewis was restored to freedom."[95] But the people of Queens were shown no mercy by Captain Archibald Hamilton. Beatings by this man were prevalent, and more than one citizen had his home invaded under Hamilton's authority.[96]

Flushing was also the staging area for British, Loyalist and Hessian troops. Benedict Arnold had recruited some of his support there after his defection to the British. The Hessian soldiers, although aptly fierce, were more concerned with keeping warm and thieving all manner of wood, including fences, trees and houses made of wood.

Life went on in Flushing. Marriages continued. British officers, particularly those who were in the navy, married local women. Property, including slaves, was bought and sold. Farmers continued to grow their produce and sell to the British when asked. The education of the young continued in traditional subjects like Latin. Religious services continued, particularly those of the Friends, or Quakers. Even though their meetinghouse had been taken over by the British for billeting and offices, the Friends held services in houses and barns. When they informed the colonel of their intention to hold meetings all over Long Island, they were granted permission.[97]

British soldiers, including the Seventy-First Highlanders and the Brigade of Loyal American Volunteers, were stationed all over Flushing. There was an indeterminate amount of soldiers quartered. Accounts in *Rivington's Gazette* and through spies were inconclusive and mostly noted soldiers' arrivals and departures. Hessians were also quartered in Flushing, as were Grenadiers and Dragoons. The majority of the British were stationed from Whitestone to Jamaica. With the numbers of British soldiers not engaged in military activities, there was a notable rise in offenses committed against the citizens.[98]

# Jamaica

Jamaica first took a poll of freeholders on March 31, 1775, in order to determine voting for deputies to the Continental Congress in May. Jamaica formed a company of Minutemen in the fall of 1775, which came with a "promise to be obedient to the officers and subject to the resolutions and directions of the Continental Congress and the Provincial Congress of the colony."[99] Jamaica has had a noteworthy reputation for those who have left legacies of courage and fortitude.

## Nathaniel Woodhull

General Nathaniel Woodhull, born in Suffolk County, was president of the Provincial Congress in New York in 1775 and also Brigadier General in Suffolk and Queens Counties in 1775. Relegated to securing cattle on Long Island—a necessary but non-frontline measure while the Battle of Long Island was raging—he was wounded, kept on two different prison ships and finally died a prisoner at New Utrecht on September 20, 1776. He is considered a soldier and Patriot of the American Revolution.[100]

## Marinus Willet

Marinus Willet was born in Jamaica in 1740 and was an ardent Patriot who became a leader of Patriots in New York City. He was part of a contingent of officers assigned to attack the Tories on Long Island. The Tories had a store of British ammunition and weapons, and it was Willet's assignment to capture the weapons. Captain Willet was an experienced Indian fighter and used their tactics when Washington's army needed weapons. His unit was to take over Jamaica, which it did. The Tories surrendered, several hundred were captured and one thousand muskets were taken, along with gunpowder and captured Tory leaders. Although this area would later be under British occupation after the Battle of Long Island, it was a major defeat for the Tories. Marinus Willet would go on to be sheriff of New York, the negotiator of a treaty with the Creek Indians during Washington's administration and mayor of New York City.[101]

## Francis Lewis

Francis Lewis was a remarkable man who could have retired prior to becoming a member of the Continental Congress and signer of the Declaration of Independence, but as with many of the Declaration's signers, his personal involvement and commitment to this cause would cost him dearly.

Lewis was a Patriot, dedicated to protesting the successive economic acts of the British government. He was a member of the Sons of Liberty in New York, and as part of the Continental Congress, he put his talents to work on a variety of committees.

After signing the Declaration of Independence, a British battleship fired on Lewis's home when his wife was there. They then attacked the home and dragged her off to a prison ship. She was eventually released and died about two years later, in declining health as a result of her incarceration.[102]

## North Hempstead

North Hempstead, as mentioned earlier, was originally part of Hempstead and subject to Tory rule. However, on September 23, 1775, a resolution was passed stating, "We be no further considered as a part of the township of Hempstead than is consistent with peace, liberty and safety; therefore in all matters relative to the Congressional plan, we shall consider ourselves as an entire, separate and independent beat or district."[103]

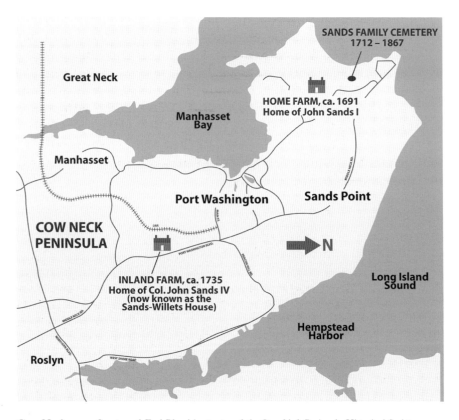

Cow Neck map. *Courtesy of Fred Blumlein, trustee of the Cow Neck Peninsula Historical Society.*

Great Neck and Cow Neck, which include the present-day Port Washington, had a strong militia that regularly drilled and trained. Captain Sands levied fines for delinquent militiamen and oversaw officers and men, including Quakers, in the district. By March 27, 1777, their section of the association had recommended that his militia unit, located in the county of Queens and colony of New York, voluntarily engage in activities to defend the American colonies against the British until such time as there was a settlement between the two countries.[104] As the Battle of Long Island loomed, the militia fortified itself against British landing of ships and troops.

After the Battle of Long Island and during occupation, family or prisoner exchange was done cautiously, and armed whaleboat attacks on Long Island by Patriots who had fled to Connecticut were conducted regularly. Cow Bay, Hempstead Harbor and Sands Points were some areas of landing for these attacks.

Farther inland, other areas such as the original Hempstead Plains, near Herricks and Westbury and later to be a famous area for historic air flights, were the scene of vandals and robbers from both sides of the Revolutionary War. Houses were robbed, livestock and valuables taken, travelers and carriages stopped and violent crimes and murders committed.[105] The occupants of those houses or the travelers who were robbed could have been Loyalist, but often assumptions were made by Patriots that if people were on Long Island after the Battle of Long Island, they were supporting or supplying the British and Hessians, either willingly or unwillingly. Oftentimes the innocent were also the victims.

## Hempstead

The Town of Hempstead was about as divisive a location as any in the colonies. Patriots and Loyalists battled legally for control of the area. In April 1775, the people of Hempstead passed a resolution stating that they "have already borne true and faithful allegiance to his Majestic King George the Third." They further stated "that it is our ardent desire to have the present unnatural contest between the parent State and her Colonies amicably and speedily accommodated" and they "will to the utmost of their power, support our legal magistrates in suppressing all riots and preserving the peace of our liege sovereign."[106]

Before the Battle of Long Island, weapons were confiscated by Continental troops. Loyalists still were able to form their own militia units and present a united defense against the Patriots. For the previous six months, Hempstead had "found itself an outlaw, not only from the province, but also from the entire thirteen colonies."[107]

The Declaration of Independence would forever change the relationship between the Patriots and the Loyalists.[108] The Loyalists of Hempstead were a "conspicuous isolation."[109]

# Oyster Bay

Oyster Bay was not only one of the areas of stationed British soldiers but also one of the places of the Long Island spy ring that is mentioned in a later chapter.

As early as 1766, Oyster Bay had declared its allegiance to King George and at the same time declared its opposition to the 1765 Stamp Act in an act of a committee of the Sons of Liberty, which were located in Oyster Bay.

Oyster Bay had a noteworthy Loyalist regiment named the Queens Rangers. The Queens Rangers were recruited from Long Island and Connecticut and became well known for their fierce fighting.[110] They had a unit stationed at Oyster Bay. The unit of Queens Rangers stationed in Oyster Bay arrived on November 19, 1778, and was under Lieutenant Colonel Simcoe. They fortified a central hill and made a redoubt filled with field pieces, men and militia.

Oyster Bay is also noted for having two historic homes that stood during the Revolutionary War: Raynham Hall and the Earle-Wightman House. Raynham Hall was the residence of the Townsend family; a son, Robert Townsend Jr., was a member of the spy ring. The Earle-Wightman House was named after Baptist ministers and is the location of the Oyster Bay Historical Society today.

There were two forts in the Oyster Bay and Jericho areas. The forts had at times a combination of Loyalist and British troops. A few of the British regiments were the Kings American Regiment at Oyster Bay, the British Legion at Jericho and the Light Dragoons at Cedar Swamp and Glen Cove. Oftentimes, civilians in these areas were at the mercy of the British troops because of the need for military support despite the ill treatment of civilians. The Queens Rangers stationed at Oyster Bay were generally more civil to

JOHN GREAVES SIMCOE,

LIEUT. COL. COMMANDANT OF THE QUEENS RANGERS.

B.1752—D.1806.

*Right*: Lieutenant Colonel John Greaves (Graves) Simcoe, commander of the Queens Rangers. *Courtesy of Digital Collections, New York Public Library.*

*Below*: Fortified hill sign, Oyster Bay. *Author photo.*

The Earle-Wightman House, Oyster Bay. *Author photo.*

civilians. Hessian soldiers, the Free Battalion and the Yeager Corps were also in the area. Some Hessian soldiers died of an epidemic and were buried in what is now the East Hillside Cemetery in Glen Head.[111]

The Town of Oyster Bay, in addition to the hamlet of Oyster Bay, included land from the North Shore of Long Island all the way to the South Shore.

## Chapter 5

# Suffolk County
# Harbors Revolutionaries

S uffolk County during the American Revolution was by no means a scene of pastoral events and beleaguered citizens who solely succumbed to British and Hessian occupation. It was a time of covert actions by Patriots and outright combat.

There was a standing committee for Suffolk County voted to be in contact with the Committee of Correspondence in New York City. This committee consisted of William Smith, Esq.; Colonel Nathaniel Woodhull; Colonel William Floyd; Mr. Thomas Fanning; Captain David Millford; and Captain Jonathan Baker. Its first correspondence would be to deal with the closing of the Port of Boston under the Coercive Acts of 1774.[112] Some of these men were also chosen later as part of the Committee of Observation and other committees pertinent to the political atmosphere of Suffolk County just prior to and during the Revolutionary War. Jonathan Baker, in June 1776, would be convicted of "taking up arms and corresponding with the British ships…Jonathan Baker was sent up to the Litchfield, CT jail."[113] Thomas Fanning "was carried off by a party of rebels in June 1778 to Connecticut."[114]

The Declaration of Independence was read on July 22, 1776, in several places around Huntington, with shouts from the people. The flag that hung on the liberty pole underwent a change. The Union Jack was cut off, and the letters "George III" were discarded. An effigy was then made of King George III and lined with gunpowder. It was exploded and

The Arsenal, Huntington. *Author's photo.*

burned.[115] After the Battle of Long Island at Brooklyn in August 1776, "the enthusiastic demonstrations of the people of Suffolk County were quickly silenced and the British took full possession of Long Island."[116]

## Whaleboats

Suffolk County experienced many whaleboat raids, particularly from Connecticut, during the Revolutionary War. Most raids had a mission of vandalism, thievery or murder against Loyalists, in particular, on Long Island. Since many Patriot refugees fled to Connecticut, there was the intention to strike at those who stayed on Long Island.

The whaleboats were about thirty feet long and pointed at both ends. They were light and silent and could easily traverse the coves on the Northern Shore of Long Island and the Southern Shore of Connecticut. Some of the inlets that they went to on Long Island were Huntington, Setauket and Port Jefferson from the inlets of Greenwich, Stamford, Norwalk and Guildford in Connecticut. The original intention of Whale-Boat Warfare was to support the privateers. They also needed to find food and provisions for the

Continental army, destroy whatever provisions of the enemy they could and also destroy British property. There were several purposes in sending covert whaleboats to Long Island from Connecticut, including obtaining provisions for the American army and depriving the British and Hessian armies of provisions by destroying grains and food and taking cattle and other useful animals. And then there was the exchange of prisoners, for which British prisoners, who could be secured by the whaleboat raids, were needed.[117]

Most of the whaleboats and whaleboat men came from Long Island, mostly as refugees who had fled to Connecticut. A British paper called them "a gang of ruffians." Many of the whaleboat trips went from Connecticut to Oyster Bay, North Hempstead and Hempstead. Their purpose was to get goods and boats.[118]

Whaleboats provided a way for the Americans to strike at the British in their own area but do it often and in a covert manner. One result of Whale-Boat Warfare was that the British would close their headquarters in Lloyd's Neck, near Huntington. Conversely, the whaleboat attacks were not just by Patriots. The British also participated, oftentimes with as much antagonism as the Patriots.[119] Whale-Boat Warfare became the impetus for the predatory excursions and the Illicit Trade mentioned in the "Commerce, British Style" chapter. There was a "spirit of adventure" developed as a result of these raids, and the military would also use these raids and boats to facilitate its own excursions. The whaleboat raids would last throughout the Revolutionary War.[120]

Long Island inhabitants, some of whom stayed only by falsely taking the oath of loyalty to King George III, were subjected to raids by those who had fled Long Island. Deacon Hedge's home, which was near Brookhaven, was robbed of wearing apparel, household goods and more.[121]

## Battles

There was another reason for whaleboat use: the battles that took place mainly in Suffolk County, an extensive area easily connected by water to Connecticut. In November 1776, almost four hundred Patriot troops came across Long Island Sound and landed at Setauket, where they encountered General Howe's troops. The Patriots returned to Connecticut with twenty-three prisoners.[122]

The Battles of Sag Harbor, Fort St. George and Fort Salonga (Slongo) are three of the noteworthy battles of Suffolk during the Revolutionary War.

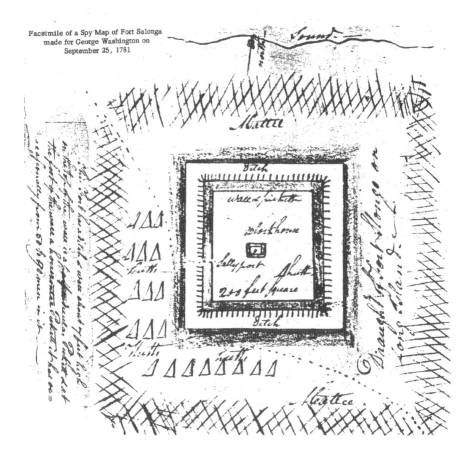

Facsimile of a Spy Map of Fort Salonga made for George Washington on September 25, 1781

Battle of Fort Slongo map. *Courtesy of the Huntington town historian.*

## The Battle of Sag Harbor and Lieutenant Colonel Return Jonathan Meigs

The Battle of Sag Harbor occurred on May 23, 1777, when Lieutenant Colonel Return Jonathan Meigs came from Guildford, Connecticut, and landed at Southold, Long Island, with 170 men. He and his men destroyed a dozen ships and provisions at Sag Harbor on the South Fork and took ninety prisoners.[123]

Return Jonathan Meigs's name was given to him after his father, Jonathan Meigs, courted his future wife, Ruth. During their courtship, he asked her many times to marry him. She kept saying, "I respect thee but I can't marry thee." Trying a different tact, he stated that he would not

52

Lieutenant Colonel Return Jonathan Meigs led the raid against the British at Sag Harbor. *Courtesy of the Long Island Collection, East Hampton Library.*

return. As he left, she kept shouting at him, "Return Jonathan!" until he came back. So they named their firstborn "Return Jonathan Meigs."[124]

## *Battle of Fort St. George*

On November 23, 1780, the battle and capture of Fort St. George took place. Rhode Island Loyalists had taken residence around the manor house

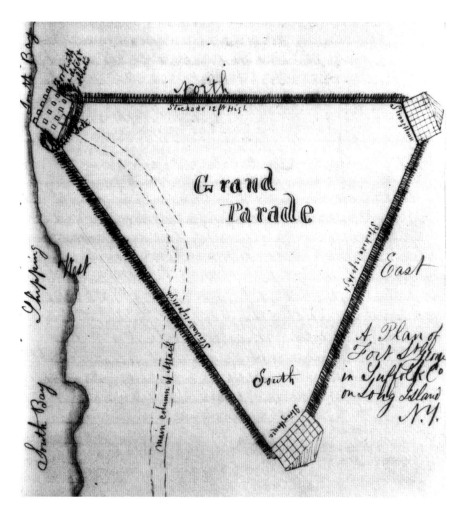

Fort St. George map. *Courtesy of the Long Island Collection, East Hampton.*

owned by General John Smith, which was located in Smith's Point on the South Shore of Long Island. The area was named Fort St. George and had a "triangular enclosure constructed by the British, with strongly barricaded houses at two angles, and the pickets projecting from the earthen mound surrounding the fort. Fifty men had been stationed there."[125]

Major Tallmadge, mentioned later in the "Spies, Patriots and Saboteurs" chapter, had crossed Long Island Sound in disguise to look at the fort. He went back and then returned on November 21, 1780, with eight of his dragoons in whaleboats, but due to weather, he had to use the overturned whaleboats for shelter that night. On the early morning of November 23, Tallmadge

Manor of St. George, Mastic. *Author's photo.*

and his men attacked the fort. Within ten minutes, the fort was captured with shouts of "Washington and his glory!" The fort was demolished, and the small vessels at the wharf were burned.[126] In a letter from Thomas T. Jackson to Sylvester Dering of Middleton, Connecticut, Jackson wrote, "[We] attacked and carried Fort George on Major William Smith's Farm in a few minutes without the loss of one man."[127]

## *Battle of Fort Salonga*

One of the last noteworthy battles on Long Island was the Battle of Fort Salonga, also called Slongo, in honor of a British officer.[128] This battle also happened quickly, with a crossing under cover darkness and an attack in the daylight. The fort, in the northwest corner of Smithtown, was occupied by 140 well-armed men. The detachment of men sent from Saugatuck, Connecticut, successfully captured the fort, killing and wounding four, taking twenty-one prisoners and destroying the fort with no loss of life and only one seriously wounded.[129]

Battle of Fort Slongo sign.

## Huntington

One of the towns with the most political activism during the American Revolution was Huntington. In June 1774, the freeholders of Huntington approved a Declaration of Rights that combatted the British right to tax the colonies without representation. This document also denounced the Coercive Acts of 1774—also called the Intolerable Acts by the colonists—which included closing the port of Boston. Along with other areas, Huntington's citizens embargoed British goods and vowed to stop trade with Britain. There were several men, including Platt Conklin, John Sloss and Thomas Wicks, whose names stand out today, that were included in committees in Suffolk County and New York City. By July 22, 1776, the town residents had heard of the Declaration of Independence (see Appendix), which was detailed in a newspaper account the next day, along with an account of the exploding of a figure of King George III wrapped in part of a British flag. On this flag, any vestiges of Britain and King George III had been torn off, while only the word "Liberty" was left. The loss of the Battle of Long Island, particularly with the Huntington militia involved, left no hope for the citizens, and Huntington was occupied. Over five hundred Huntington residents, in an act of desperation to hold on to land and possessions, signed

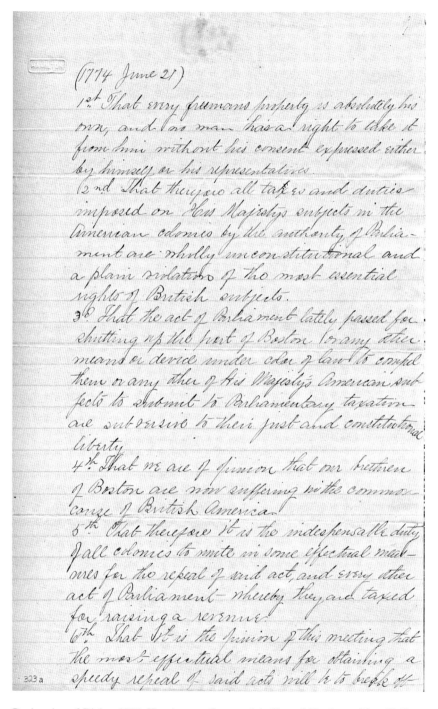

(1774 June 21)

1st. That every freemans property is absolutely his own, and no man has a right to take it from him without his consent expressed either by himself or his representatives.

2nd. That therefore all taxes and duties imposed on His Majestys subjects in the American colonies by the authority of Parliament are wholly unconstitutional and a plain violation of the most essential rights of British subjects.

3d. That the act of Parliament lately passed for shutting up the port of Boston or any other means or device under color of law to compel them or any other of His Majesty's American subjects to submit to Parliamentary taxation are subversive to their just and constitutional liberty.

4th. That we are of opinion that our brethren of Boston are now suffering in the common cause of British America.

5th. That therefore it is the indispensable duty of all colonies to unite in some effectual measures for the repeal of said act, and every other act of Parliament whereby they are taxed for raising a revenue.

6th. That it is the opinion of this meeting that the most effectual means for obtaining a speedy repeal of said acts will be to break off

303 a

Declaration of Rights, 1774, Huntington. *Courtesy of the Town of Huntington, Town Clerk's Record Center and Archives.*

oaths of loyalty to Britain and the king. The verbal and physical combat became a campaign of guerrilla warfare between Patriots and Loyalists from the years 1776 to 1783, when the British finally evacuated Long Island. "Nathan Rose, Benjamin Strong, Selah Strong, Samuel Thompson, and others were all officers in the army."[130] Some of these men will be covered in another chapter.

The companies of militia were strong in numbers. In the Eastern Regiment, 768 officers and privates were raised. East Hampton supplied two of the companies. Bridge Hampton supplied two companies, and Sag Harbor supplied two more. These three areas—Bridge Hampton, East Hampton and Southampton—all supplied companies of Minutemen to guard the homefront in their areas.[131]

In the Western Regiment, there were thirteen companies that included 1,030 officers and men. The companies came from Huntington, Brookhaven, Smithtown, Islip and Southold.[132]

## GENERAL NATHANIEL WOODHULL

General Nathaniel Woodhull was born in Mastic, Long Island, in December 1722. As with many notable families, there was intermarriage, and his wife was the sister of Colonel William Floyd. General Woodhull was head of the

The Abraham Woodhull home. *Courtesy of the Long Island Collection, East Hampton Library.*

58

delegation from Suffolk that met in New York City in May 1775. He served as Colonel and was appointed Brigadier General of the Brigade of Militia formed from Suffolk and Queens Counties.[133] He was active in his military duties in Jamaica as of August 1776. After the Battle of Long Island, one of the threats was the loss of cattle, which were herded in Montauk, the Hempstead Plains and other fields. The livestock were a needed commodity to the British, and the British were now tasked with capturing and cornering Woodhull's command. Woodhull was captured at the tavern of Increase Carpenter. When Woodhull refused to comply with a British officer's demand to say, "God save the king," instead saying, "God save us all," the officer pierced Woodhull with his sword. Woodhull was taken to a church in Jamaica and, the next day, to a prison ship in Gravesend Bay. Infection set into his wounds, and he died on September 20, 1776.[134]

## Colonel William Floyd

William Floyd was also born in Mastic. He lived from 1734 to 1821; his last home was in Westerville, New York.

*On September 5, 1775 William Floyd was nominated colonel of the Western Regiment of Suffolk County at a meeting in Smithtown. Suffolk County elected Floyd to the Continental Congress on April 22, 1775… The Floyds settled at Middletown, Connecticut (after the Battle of Yorktown).*[135]

He was not only a New York signer of the Declaration of Independence but also a Long Islander!

The Floyds' four-thousand-acre estate in Mastic had been seized, and even though William Floyd's wife and children were safely

William Floyd, signer of the Declaration of Independence. *Courtesy of the Eastern National Park & Monument Association. Reproduction of a 1792 painting by Ralph Earl (postcard).*

resettled in Connecticut, she died in 1781 from hardship at the age of forty-one. He would return in 1783 to rebuild the home, which had been destroyed by the British.[136]

He had been actively involved in reporting activities of the war, even from a distance in Connecticut. He had remained a Patriot despite severe circumstances faced by himself and his family.

## Colonel Josiah Smith

Colonel Josiah Smith was born in East Moriches, Long Island, in November 1723 and appointed a Colonel of the regiment of Minute Men when the Revolutionary War began. He went on to organize the Suffolk County regiment, which consisted of about four hundred men and was considered the best trained on Long Island. These men participated in the Battle of Long Island, but when the battle was lost, their regiment was disbanded, and Smith "gave leave for every man to shift for himself in getting their families and effects off Long Island." He also went to Connecticut.[137]

*Chapter 6*

# Church and Politics Take Sides

O n July 8, 1776, the Continental Congress declared, "Whereas the
Continental Congress have recommended to the inhabitants of the
colonies to keep the 20th of July, instant, as a day of Fasting and Prayer, this
Congress does strictly enjoin all persons in this colony religiously to observe
the same."[138]

Churches were the mainstays of life in a community. But political
affiliations and predilections were inevitable, particularly during a time of
imminent war and occupation.

Churches on Long Island during the American Revolution were used as
houses of worship but were often ransacked by the British and also used
as political venues by Patriot ministers. The churches oftentimes became a
point of desecration if they were "not of the established faith [of the British
Church of England or High Episcopal]—were mostly occupied by soldiers,
or used as store houses and for prisoners; some were even torn down."[139]

There was a division of church existence in the colonies that originated
in England. Many of the differences in religious existence in the colonies
filtered into Long Island as well. New England had early religious
controversies based on the fact that many colonies had religious-specific
environments. There were many Presbyterians on Long Island who had
been Congregationalists in New England. In some of the churches, such
as in Connecticut, Congregationalists adopted other religions' hierarchical
structures, with pastors, elders and deacons. So some of the churches still
adhered to the structure of the churches in England while others changed

their church leadership to fit the geographical environment they were in. This would lead to churches either being accepted or rejected by the British during the Revolutionary War.[140]

## Church of England

Migration from New England to Long Island was generally because of religion. Long Island had several main religions, but most prominent was Episcopal, which was favored by officials and oftentimes given financial support by the government.

Hempstead was the location of the first Episcopal church.[141]

> *Churches and places for religious worship were desecrated for any objects which suited the commerce of the enemy, except those of the Episcopalians, which were, it seems scrupulously regarded, doubtless in pursuance of governmental instructions, their members* [on Long Island] *being in general in the interests of England.*[142]

Many of the Presbyterian and Dutch churches were used for riding schools, hospitals, billeting of soldiers and other uses. Some churches in Huntington and Babylon were torn down, and the materials from the buildings were used to build barracks and stables, among other buildings.[143] There was also suspicion of the Church of England in America. As a representative of Britain, this church came under scrutiny even during the years prior to the Revolutionary War when the colonies were facing economic or political acts set against them and began combatting these acts in their own covert or overt ways. This church, as a whole, wanted to bring all of the English subjects into a community. Although toleration of other religions was allowed, there was a great attempt—at least covertly—to create an official church in America. One means of doing this was the Society of the Propagation of the Gospel in Foreign Parts, which was created in 1701 to proselytize to the Indians and, by 1763, to root out Presbyterianism and establish episcopacy.[144]

# THE FIRST REFORMED CHURCH OF FLATBUSH

The First Reformed Church of Flatbush began in 1654 under the Church of Holland. The church had people from surrounding areas come to worship under men who were brought in. But travel was often difficult to the church. "The people living in the three villages of Brooklyn, Flatbush, and Flatlands come with great difficulty to the preaching here [New York]…It was some three hours work for some of them ere to reach here."[145] The area chosen for the church in Flatbush (originally called Midout) was due to its geographical location and accessibility. A list of pastors reveals many who were paternal in nature and respected in their preaching, although none was listed as having served during the Revolutionary War. The Dutch Reformed Church was changed to the Reformed Church in America in 1867.

*In 1774 a lottery was proposed for the creation of a church comfortable to the doctrines of the Church of England, but the matter was either unsuccessful or was allowed to be dropped owing to the political exigencies of the times. During the British occupation there is no doubt Episcopalian services were held and some of the discourses preached by the Rev. James Sayre are still preserved. It was not until 1784 until the cloud of battle had passed away, that those who adhered to the Episcopalian Church set up a tabernacle of their own. It scarcely took the form of a church: there were few, very few Episcopalians in this town or country at that period.[146]*

# BROOKLYN

The Flatbush Dutch Reformed Church was part of the first settlement in Flatbush about 1699. The same small church building was still there during the Revolutionary War. There was a bell rope that hung down and gave first warning of the British landing before the Battle of Long Island. The church became a temporary hospital after the battle and then became a stable for British horses.[147]

"During the war of the Revolution, the British officers held divine service, according to their own forms, in the Dutch churches, the Rev. James Sayre officiating from 1778–1783."[148]

"The wounded prisoners taken, August 27 [during the Battle of Long Island], were put in the churches of Flatbush and N. Utrecht, but being neglected and unattended, were wallowing in their own filth, and breathed an infected air."[149]

## CHURCHES: SUFFOLK COUNTY

There were many churches that served the colonial population on Long Island and were either of use during the American Revolutionary War and occupation or were vandalized, misused or destroyed in some manner.

### Caroline Church, Setauket

Caroline Church had its start as Christ Church. It was renamed in honor of Queen Caroline, the wife of George II, when she donated a silver communion service and altar cloths to the church. When the Battle of Setauket took place on August 22, 1777, the wounded were taken care of in the church building. It had a history during the war of both use and possible

Caroline Church, Setauket. *Courtesy of Three-Village Historical Society.*

Setauket Village Green sign, Setauket. *Author's photo.*

abuse. The British left it intact, but it was also supposedly used as a barracks at one point.[150]

Caroline Church is the oldest church on Long Island that is still standing. It had a gallery added in 1744, and it also provided pews in the back for slaves that have been called the "slave gallery."[151]

## Presbyterian Church in Middle Island

This church was built in 1766 in an area then called Middletown, and its pastor, Reverend David Rose, was also pastor of the Presbyterian Church at South Haven, Connecticut, through the pre-Revolutionary period and Revolutionary War until his death in 1799. Reverend Rose, called "Priest Rose," was a Patriot supporter of the American Revolution and served with Colonel Josiah Smith at the Battle of Long Island in August 1776.[152] His family was sent, like many other Long Islanders, to Connecticut for protection. During the Revolutionary War, the churches were used by the British as barracks and a horse stable. There were no services held during the war years, and Reverend Rose had to restore both churches, as well as gather congregations after the war.[153]

## Other Churches

There were other churches. Some of these were the first Baptist Church in Brookhaven Town, built in Coram in 1747; the Congregational Church in Mount Sinai before the one in 1789; and a Presbyterian meetinghouse in Wading River.

## *Huntington Church*

Huntington was one of the towns that particularly suffered during the Revolutionary War:

> *The church pews* [were] *torn up, the sacred edifice was converted into a military depot, and afterwards entirely pulled down; the timber was used to construct barracks and block houses.*

The burying ground was renamed Fort Golgotha by the British, and headstones were knocked over and used for baking. Bread that was baked on the turned-over headstones would have the epitaphs of friends of the deceased on the bottom crust.[154]

Old Burying Ground, seventeenth century, where Fort Golgotha was erected. *Author's photo.*

GOLGOTHA – A PROVINCIAL FORT

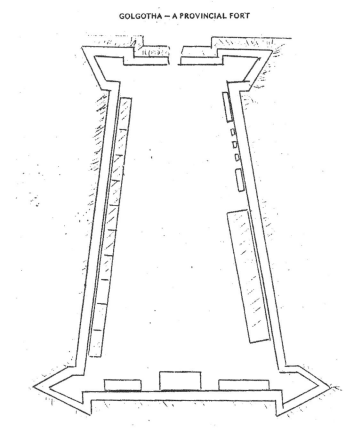

Fort Golgotha map for the Old Burying Ground. *Courtesy of the Huntington town historian.*

## Reverend Samuel Buel

Reverend Buel was well liked by the British and Governor Tryon. "He frequently joined the parties of the British officers, which he enlivened by humorous anecdotes and agreeable conversation." On one occasion, Reverend Buel responded to a British officer's intense remark of commanding "a legion of devils just from hell" by stating that he must be addressing the "prince of devils." The officer was not initially amused, but after careful cajoling by Reverend Buel, he soon had a change of heart.[155]

Reverend Buel was "an able divine, excellent pastor. [He] delivered ten thousand sermons and died at eighty-two years old."[156]

## Reverend Ebenezer Prime

By 1773, Huntington, like all areas, had been experiencing the struggle for independence. Reverend Prime, having been the assistant to the pastor in Huntington when he was nineteen, went on to be the only pastor up until his age made serving the people difficult. He was forced to flee his home and hide his possessions from the British. He was particularly hated by Colonel Rumford, who had allowed all manner of degradation against the church and burying ground. When the British officers took possession of Reverend Prime's home, they destroyed books and valuables. After Reverend Prime died in 1779, Colonel Rumford "pitched a tent behind this old pastor's grave," stating "that he would have the pleasure every time he went out of treading on the old rebel."[157]

# CHURCHES IN QUEENS COUNTY

Queens County had a mixture of prominent faiths in its history. Between the 1760s and the end of the 1800s, many different congregations were in Jamaica. The Episcopalians were already established, and the German Reformed Methodists had developed a strong presence by the Revolutionary era. In the later 1600s, a stone church had been built in Jamaica by the Presbyterians, who were the main denomination. By 1700, Presbyterianism was no longer the main religion, and at the same time, there were attempts to enforce an English set of statutes that conformed to the Anglican Church. When this did not work, the British governor seized the church property. During the occupation of Long Island, the stone church served as a British military prison for Patriot prisoners.[158]

## St. George's Church (Episcopal)

The rectors of St. George's Church were Samuel Seabury from 1742 to 1764, serving twenty-two years, and Leonard Cutting from 1766 to 1783, serving seventeen years. By January 1776, Mr. Cutting had stated that there was "political turmoil, which was upheaving the country, and whose unhappy effects were to be felt more and more by the parish, but not by means to such an extent as by many others in our country."[159]

The church was closed for three Sundays before the British arrived. By January 1777, Mr. Cutting had stated in a letter that St. George's Church fared better than most churches under occupation. The congregants had been subjected to harassment by Patriots since most of the people in that area were Loyalists. When the British occupied Long Island, this congregation was content. However, it was the only church in the area that was allowed to operate as a church, so it was particularly vulnerable to Patriot attacks.[160]

St. George's Church, Hempstead. *Author's photo.*

## Grace Church, Jamaica, Queens

Until 1766, Reverend Samuel Seabury was rector of Grace Church. Reverend Seabury was a Loyalist and distinguished clergy as bishop of Connecticut. He was made a prisoner in New Haven by the Patriots around 1777, but by 1778, he was in the ministry in Staten Island until 1782.[161]

From 1769 to 1790, including the crucial years of Long Island occupation by the British, Reverend Joshua Bloomer oversaw three congregations, including Jamaica, Newtown and Flushing. Many of his congregants during the Revolution were arrested and had property confiscated. Reverend Bloomer attempted to minister to his congregations during the period of arrests and imprisonments by Patriots. During this time, he was not allowed to pray for the king and his family. The church was shut down for five Sundays as a result until the British troops arrived to occupy Long Island. Then services were resumed, and attendance went from five to sixty-six; Reverend Bloomer baptized infants and adults and married couples. His last report was in 1781.[162]

## Quaker Meetinghouse

In the 1690s, the Friends, or Quakers, established a house of worship after meeting in their homes. By August 28, 1777, when the Battle of Long Island was lost, Flushing, Long Island, also succumbed to occupation. The British soldiers would billet in houses and use churches for military purposes. "The Quaker Meeting house in Flushing was used as a prison, a hospital, and a hay magazine." The Quakers were in the midst of a meeting when the British came to take possession of their place of worship, but the British waited until the Quakers were leaving to do this. The Quakers did not officially support either side of the war and suffered from loss of property to both sides as a result. There were some Quakers who were suspected of aiding the Patriots, and an official order was issued that those people would be fined for noncompliance, or conversely, those Quakers who "held fast to their integrity" and did not aid the Patriots would be shown lenience.[163]

In a letter written by Hessian officer Ambrose Serle in April 1777, he stated that the inhabitants of Long Island "are accepting a few Presbyterians to the Eastward, eminent for their loyalty." A few months later, concerning the attitude of the Quakers in Flushing, Serle noted, "The Quakers are not rebels; on the contrary they have publicly

Quaker Meetinghouse, Flushing. *William Dyer, artist, postcard.*

proclaimed in all their gatherings and churches that whosoever went armed would lose their membership."[164]

Other Quaker meetinghouses are in Manhasset, Farmingdale-Bethpage, Westbury and Oyster Bay, among others.

## Quakers

The earliest meetinghouse was in the "Oyster Bay Township which was the center of activity for Quakers for many years on Long Island, owing to the zeal and work of Elias Hicks, a most remarkable man."[165] In fact, the Hicks name is still prominent in the Westbury area.

## Manhasset

*In 1782 the Meeting House in Manhasset was occupied by Hessian Cavalrymen. The Friends protested to the English Governor-General Robertson, who ordered Colonel Wormb to vacate and restore the building. In 1783 it was again occupied by soldiers as a guard house and considerable damage was done to the seats and fence which had to be repaired by the Meeting, as the British and Hessians were shortly forced to withdraw from the Island.*[166]

## Westbury

The Yeagers (Hessians) had camps at Westbury, where they attended the Friends Meeting House and "sat very commendable."

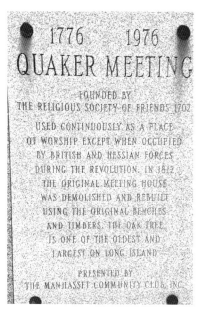

A Quaker meetinghouse sign, Manhasset. The original building on this site was occupied by the British and Hessians. *Author's photo.*

*Cahpter 7*

# Commerce, British Style

## THE CONTINENTAL ASSOCIATION

Prior to the pre-Revolutionary years of 1763–75, the British dominated colonial trade. Then, during the pre-Revolutionary years, political and economic oppression would lead to the formulation of the Continental Congress under a Continental Association (see Appendix).

John Dickinson wrote a series of pamphlets under the name *Letters from a Pennsylvania Farmer* in a practical manner for anyone to read. The colonies were under English law but were being subjected to harsher treatment, and he wrote about the colonists resisting the increasingly punitive British taxes, particularly the Townshend duties, between 1763 and 1775. He wrote, "If Parliament could levy a duty on colonial imports, England might, out of selfish considerations, overtax any and all American articles," and in that event, "the tragedy of American Liberty would be finished."[167] These acts were not only increasingly unbearable financially but socially as well. Long Island, among other areas, would be forced to house British soldiers while under occupation, even though New York refused to obey the 1765 Quartering Act. New York also abided by a colonial non-importation agreement of British goods until the overwhelming taxes were repealed. The only problem was that trade with Great Britain was also lessened, and this was one of the main issues between Patriots and Loyalists.

*In part the* [Continental] *Association was the standardization and nationalization of the systems of commercial opposition which had hitherto been employed upon a local scale; the earlier experiments in non-importation, non-consumption, and various forms of the secondary boycott bore fruit in a number of carefully drawn provisions of the Association.*[168]

In the Continental Association, the members "entered into solemn pledge in behalf of themselves and their constituents not to import goods from England after December 1, 1774, nor to export any of their own commodities except rice to the British Isles after September 10, 1775."[169] This was an agreement throughout the colonies and one of the most successful. It was said that "the people were more obedient to its provisions than they were to the laws of the provincial legislatures."[170] What is amazing is that the system of communication became structured around committees of correspondence that were like an intricate web binding the colonies together. The committees were local, such as out on Long Island, and then representative of the colony, such as in New York City, which would receive information from the local area. "By the middle of 1773 six colonies were linked by committees of correspondence."[171]

It was no easy task getting all thirteen colonies to agree on features of the Continental Association. On Long Island, Suffolk County, which included central and eastern Long Island, was in agreement with the association, while Queens County was deeply divided over it.[172]

Of the fourteen articles of the association, three were in reference to non-importation and non-exportation. The non-importation of British goods, which went into effect on December 1, 1774, included molasses, syrups and coffee.[173]

## Long Island as a Commercial Prize

Even though there was an occupation in place and goods were basically embargoed, Long Island was rich in stores of goods, natural resources and animals that were already here:

*Long Island was a valuable prize of war. The inhabitants of its three counties reportedly paid two-thirds of the colonial taxes. The surrounding waters yielded shellfish of all kinds and quantities of fish; field and forest furnished wild fowl of all sorts. In exchange for British merchandise the country people bartered hogs calves, hams, lambs, poultry and smoked beef; they probably welcomed hard money from the foe for planks, boards, and shingles.*[174]

There was an advantage to a smaller property. Oftentimes, people had to watch their possessions and animals by sleeping with them in the same room. "It was no uncommon thing for a farmer, his wife and children, to sleep in one room, while his sheep were bleating in the adjoining, his hogs grunting in the kitchen, the cock crowing, hens cackling, ducks quacking and geese hissing, in the cellar."[175]

On a larger scale, Long Island had a huge shipbuilding industry, particularly between the years 1750 and 1820. Its many caves and inlets were excellent protected areas for building and docking.[176] Later, Long Island would also be one of the centers for shipbuilding during World War II in the Brooklyn Navy Yard.

## Theirs for the "Taking"

As occupation took place, the valuable commodities of goods and animals would become more and more important to the British and Hessians.

> *The inhabitants* [of Long Island] *could not go from the city, or bring out goods, without a permit. The price of wood and farmers produce was regulated by proclamation; their horses, wagons and persons, could at any time be impressed into the King's service, at a stipulated price. In the winter season almost every village and hamlet was filled with British soldiers and wagoners, billeted in people's houses, or cantoned in temporary huts. The consequence was a ready market and high price for such of the farmer's produce as had not been previously pilfered.*[177]

Long Island had a large herd of cattle and sheep—approximately 100,000 of each, which were mainly in Kings County and out in Montauk. Patriot Whigs did not want the herds to fall into enemy hands and had them driven from the coasts to different areas inland. If necessary, the animals would be destroyed. General Nathaniel Woodhull, who later perished from wounds and ill treatment by the British, was put in charge of this operation. Approximately 1,400 cattle were herded into Hempstead with not enough soldiers to oversee them.[178]

By the spring of 1778, when the British troops went farther east than Jamaica, the army was in need of cattle. Mrs. William Floyd wrote of the economic suffering of her friends when the British killed at least ten cattle a day to feed the soldiers.[179] Sometimes receipts were given for commodities like animals taken and sometimes not. Farmers were one main group that sold food, crops and animals to whatever side of the war needed them. But "the Long Island people were selling off their small cattle and poultry, as they were daily robbed of them by the soldiers."[180] There were

*insatiable demands for timber, foodstuffs, and other supplies* [which] *exhausted supplies and produced scarcity. British officers requisitioned cattle, wood, forage, and fresh provisions from Island farmers, who had no other outlet for sale, and confiscated boats, mills, and arms in Suffolk. What these officers did not purchase was plundered by British soldiers, who stripped farmers of their foodstuffs, drink, and horses. Both Loyalists and Patriots were victims, because their families and their customers were denied what they needed for survival.*[181]

As part of colonial life, certain hardwood trees—such as black locust of a particular circumference on Long Island—were forbidden to be cut down by the colonists because the British needed them for masts for their ships. But during the Revolutionary War, the tree forests were almost decimated. "At the end of the war no tree on Long Island over six inches in circumference was left standing except the Great Oak in Lloyd Neck. Most fences and orchards were also used as firewood by the British troops in Huntington and New York City."[182] Long Island was like one big supply depot for the British. Its geographic location as an island gave it a more secure position in maintaining its crops, animals and natural resources. Records were kept of what each farmer owned, including wagons and the dimensions of their property. At times, farmers and their sons were impressed into driving the wagons, and at other times they did it to safeguard their property.[183]

Patriots and Loyalists were subject to confiscation of property. When Patriots vacated their homes and property, the British moved through their areas to take what they needed. The British soldiers were told to "take into custody of all the grain, forage, and creatures they could find on Long Island being property of persons actually in rebellion or who have deserted their habitations." Loyalists were sent a notice to identify and reclaim animals that were taken or receive certificates for future payment, but many were not compensated.[184]

Even though a lot of the fighting moved to the southern colonies-turned-states, by 1780, Long Island was still experiencing hardship from British occupation. General Clinton's army went into winter quarters in different areas, mostly in Queens. Flushing, Jamaica and Newtown all experienced the robbing and pillaging of animals and any other commodity that could be used as a staple. Turkeys, ducks and other fowl had to be hidden at night. People attempted to protect their fields from the pillaging of the British. Larger animals like pigs were taken into the houses; people were sleeping in the same areas as their barnyard animals.[185]

Although Loyalist Long Island farmers did not want to support the Revolution, they were not always ready to support the king's troops either. Because Long Island was one of the main sources of supplies for troops below Patriot New England, there was a continual demand for all supplies for the military. When there was resistance to goods being taken and disbursed, leaving colonists with very little for themselves, General Clinton issued an order: "Farmers are ordered to thrash out immediately one third of their present crop of wheat and rye; and one third by February next; the residue by May 1. Whoever disobeys will be imprisoned and his crop confiscated."[186]

The cross-south whaleboat raids and covert actions went in both directions. Just as the Patriots raided Long Island, the Loyalist militias raided Connecticut. But the covert actions on the part of the Patriots also helped to spirit away cattle to Connecticut to keep them out of British hands.[187] The ready store of supplies was seriously depleted during the war. The cattle in Hempstead Plains dwindled. Unharvested grain was meant for the military alone. Farm equipment often was confiscated and used for other uses, such as road repair, without any hope of the owner of the equipment being reimbursed.[188] As was mentioned, buildings such as churches—like the second Presbyterian/Congregational Church in Huntington—were put to other uses or torn down and used to build Fort Golgotha, a British encampment on the Old Burying Ground.[189] This fort, also called "Fort of the Skulls," was used by the Queens Rangers and Tarleton's Legion and held about five hundred men.[190]

So there were economic consequences for the inhabitants of Long Island, and life was disrupted. Markets that had been structured were no longer. Unemployment was widespread. Both sides of the war were in search of provisions for their militaries.[191] Refugee citizens either stayed on Long Island or fled to other areas, often returning when other situations were worse than what they had left. Prices for goods and food were elevated. Life would not return to some kind of normality until well after the war was over, and then oftentimes it took years for forests, crops and provisions to return to prewar amounts.

*During the whole war the inhabitants of the island, especially those of Suffolk County, were perpetually exposed to the grossest insult and abuse. They had not property of a movable kind; properly speaking, to call their own; they were often times deprived of the stock necessary to the management of their farms and were deterred from producing more than a bare subsistence by the apprehension that a surplus would be wrested from them either by the military authority of the purveyor or the ruffian hand of the plunderer.[192]*

Looting was a lifestyle for the occupying army but also for the Patriots. Sometimes called "marauding," it was oftentimes an outcropping of the war on a civilian population, friend or foe, as much as for theft of possessions. George Washington repeatedly issued orders forbidding looting and called for strict punishment of individuals if it were discovered. The British and Hessians both considered Long Island a gold mine and theirs for the taking in order to get rich. Eventually, Sir William Howe issued orders of punishment for soldiers caught looting. After the Battle of Trenton, when almost one thousand Hessians were captured, George Washington and his men found many possessions that had been looted from New Jersey.[193]

## GRISTMILLS

Besides farming, timber and fishing, Long Island had gristmills to facilitate the use of grains for food. Saddle Rock Gristmill in Great Neck was built in 1700, the Roslyn Gristmill between the years

Stony Brook Gristmill, Stony Brook. The British took grains ground here during the Revolutionary War to feed their soldiers. *Author's photo.*

Saddle Rock Gristmill, village of Great Neck. *Courtesy of the Great Neck Library.*

1715 and 1745 and the East Rockaway Gristmill and the Stony Brook Gristmill in 1751. These were some of the gristmills the British used for both the product and the commerce during occupation.

## SMUGGLING, COVERT TRIPS AND TRADE

Smuggling on Long Island remained a problem for the British as early as the Molasses Act of 1733, when colonists attempted to avoid the taxes by smuggling. One of the pre-Revolutionary-era economic acts, the Sugar Act of 1764, cut the tax of the Molasses Act in half. Long Island was perfect for smuggling with its caves and inlets.

> *From that moment* [the abandonment of Long Island] *the two coasts* [Long Island and Connecticut] *were hostile: and an inveterate system of smuggling, marauding, plundering, and kidnapping took place on both sides in comparison with which a common state of honorable warfare might be taken for peace and good neighborhood. On the Connecticut side this was done under the covert of secrecy.*[194]

So there developed a different and separate practice during the Revolutionary War called "Predatory Excursions." These Predatory Excursions were covert trips to Long Island by refugees who had fled to Connecticut after the Battle of Long Island to strike at the people still on Long Island, whether citizen or soldier. Even if someone were a covert Patriot, there might have been an attack anyway—if people were still here, then there was a good chance that they harbored some kind of loyalty to the Crown.

Once refugees settled in Connecticut, it was up to the Authority and Selectmen of towns such as Guilford and Haddam to give permission for people to return to Long Island. When the trips back to Long Island were temporary and just as an attack on an area or person(s) or for theft, vandalism, kidnapping or guerrilla warfare, they were Predatory Excursions. People returning for civil purposes to Long Island could be granted permission by Selectmen "to carry on any kind of provision of stores for voyages, nor to bring off any British goods or merchandise."[195]

The practice of attacking Long Island for plunder or harassment was opposed by the New York legislature. A resolution was passed "requesting Gov. Clinton to issue a Proclamation forbidding all persons to plunder the inhabitants of Long Island, or any locality in the power of the enemy. It was declared that any offender should be punished to the utmost rigor of the law."[196] The ability to transit back to Long Island for goods and sundries began in 1777. Connecticut established a security measure through a fort commandant, boat overseer or other official to ensure that no goods were brought to Long Island or that there were legitimate reasons for someone to traverse the Long Island Sound and return.

*May 22, 1779. Voted. That Colo. John Hulbert, Theophilus Halsey, [Lieutenant] David Sayer [Sayre] and [Captain] Stephen Howel, be permitted to pass with a boat to Long Island and to ring off some grain, provided they first apply to Capt. [John Jr.] Shipman, commandant of the fort at Say Brook, to search said boat and see that no goods, provisions or money are on board at the time of her departure, and that on their return they shall exhibit to said Shipman a true manifest of the grain they shall have brought from said Long Island on board that boat.*[197]

*Nov. 3, 1779. Elias Howell, a refugee from Long Island, is permitted to go to Long Island and to return again, under the inspection and direction of the commandant of the fort at Saybrook. Onderdonk's "Suffolk Co, p, 103:*

*"Elias Howell, at Saybrook, May 22 81" wishes to return with family and family stores, to his aged father on L.I.*[198]

There was also a practice called "the Illicit Trade." The Illicit Trade consisted of buying imported goods in New York City, professedly for pro-British customers; carrying the same to Long Island; smuggling them over to Connecticut or Long Island; and "through a secret meeting with a boat out from New York City an exchange of provisions for English goods was made."[199]

One of the issues with the Illicit Trade was the concern that the goods would either be for the enemy or wind up in the hands of the enemy. Licenses were revoked because the permissions given were used to "carry on a clandestine and Illicit Trade with the enemies of the United States, and to keep up an unwarrantable and dangerous intercourse with them."[200]

The Predatory Excursions and the Illicit Trade were operated along Patriot and Loyalist lines. When the British needed supplies or animals, they allowed these trips to go on. George Washington definitely disapproved of the Illicit Trade. And after the fighting ended in October 1781, a New York law was passed to officially end the Illicit Trade.

Privateering was another mode of commerce originating during the French and Indian War and extending into the Revolutionary War. Privately owned vessels were licensed by the Continental Congress to acquire information about British operations. The different committees of Congress, including the Committee of Safety and the Marine Committee, oversaw the operations of the privateers.

Continental ships were outfitted and used by the Americans as a way of patrolling the waters, particularly around Long Island, and capturing enemy ships, which were sold as "prizes" or had their stores of goods sold as prizes. Two of the ships were the *Montgomery* and the *Schuyler*. And there were also American ships taken by British privateers. "Capt. Enen Dayton, on the sloop *Ranger*, 45 men and 6 guns, taken in South Bay by a British Privateer Nov. 20, 1778, and carried to N.Y. City."[201]

# OCCUPIED HOUSES

Once occupation happened in 1776, many homes were occupied by soldiers, particularly by British officers and their aides and at times by Patriot forces. They were used as headquarters and for billeting. In this

The William Floyd Estate, Mastic. *Courtesy of Prints and Photographs, Library of Congress.*

way, barracks or extra buildings for living did not have to be built. Since the homes chosen to be occupied would also have been furnished and generally had provisions, they were perfect until the war ended and evacuation occurred in December 1783.

The homes that were chosen allowed officers and aides to occupy the best rooms on the first floor while allowing families to occupy the second and third floors or attic. Both Patriot and Loyalist homes were occupied.

# Rock Hall

Rock Hall in Lawrence was one of the Loyalist areas occupied in what was then Queens County. As a home on the South Shore of Long Island, it had been newly built for Loyalist Josiah Martin, who was both seventy years old and from a very prominent family. The home had been built with many outbuildings, including slave quarters. The house occupancy swelled with people when relatives from Patriot North Carolina, the colonial governor and his family, also moved in.

As Queens County voted not to participate in the Provincial Congress, the Martin home became a takeover area for Patriot forces. The militia used this lavish home as a barracks on the first floor, taking souvenirs of their stay and hidden weapons and generally creating a crass environment and wreaking havoc on the family while they occupied the house only a short time.[202]

# Raynham Hall

Raynham Hall in Oyster Bay, also mentioned in the "Spies, Patriots and Saboteurs" chapter, was a seat of occupation by the Queens Rangers. Raynham Hall has undergone additions and changes to its historic structure but has been renovated, at least from the street view, to resemble its 1700s appearance.

Raynham Hall was built about 1740 and was the home of the Townsend family, descendants of the Townsends of Norfolk, England, after whom Raynham Hall is named. Samuel Townsend was a Quaker, a Whig, a member of the First Provincial Congress and, in 1776, a member of the committee that drafted the New York Constitution, as was requested by the Continental Congress to be done in every state.

Raynham Hall Museum, Oyster Bay. *Author's photo.*

Raynham Hall sign. *Author's photo.*

As a Quaker, Samuel Townsend did not actively oppose the British, and because he was a Whig, he and his family had to live in their home while it was occupied by officers of the Queens Rangers. Lieutenant Colonel Simcoe developed affection for Samuel's daughter Sarah, commonly called Sally. Simcoe composed what is considered to be the first valentine to Sally. Lieutenant Colonel Simcoe finally left, and Sally never married. Both Townsend daughters inspired their names to be scratched by a diamond in glass panes in their house at Raynham Hall.

Another person of historical interest who apparently stayed at Raynham Hall prior to his fateful connection to Benedict Arnold and the attempted takeover of West Point was Major Andre.[203]

# The Arsenal

The arsenal in Huntington had strong Patriot support prior to the occupation of the British on September 1, 1776. But the men who left from the arsenal to fight in the Battle of Long Island fought valiantly. At the time of the American Revolution, the arsenal was owned by Job

Sammis, a weaver who lived and worked in this home-turned-arsenal for forty-one years.

The arsenal was the beginning of the valiant effort by the Suffolk County militia to engage in the Battle of Long Island. It was the staging point for the militia to leave for the Battle of Long Island with the store of weapons and ammunition stored in Sammis's home.

After the loss of the Battle of Long Island and the takeover of Huntington, among many other towns on Long Island, Job Sammis's house was occupied by the British, along with many other homes in the area. The quartering of soldiers in people's homes was allowed by two different British Quartering Acts in the immediate pre-Revolutionary era. Like many Long Islanders, Job Sammis was forced to provide transportation in his wagons for the British supplies and theft of animals and other possessions.

## Sagtikos Manor

Sagtikos Manor in Bayshore was built in the early 1690s and has some of the original portion of the house still intact. Judge Isaac Thompson oversaw the Revolutionary era in the house and was active in the Long Island militia, including being chairman of the Islip Committee.

Sagtikos Manor, Bayshore. *Courtesy of the Sagtikos Manor Historical Society.*

Sagtikos Manor was occupied by the British on different occasions. In 1777, over three hundred British encamped around the manor house, with officers freely staying in the manor whenever they wanted. On another occasion, British sailors attacked the house at night. It was said that as Judge Thompson was going up to the third floor, where he was staying, he had a lantern in his hand and was thought by the British soldiers to be signaling someone out on the water. One of the British soldiers shot at him through a window but missed, and the bullet is still embedded in the stairwell. The manor house was robbed on another occasion, and Judge Thompson was dragged out to the road by a rope around his neck. He was released in deference to his position as Magistrate.[204]

# William Floyd Estate

William Floyd, a colonel in the Revolutionary War, was away from his home in Mastic on Long Island for most of the six years that he participated in the

The William Floyd Estate, Mastic. *Courtesy of the William Floyd estate, FINS.*

war. Colonel Floyd was a well-known Patriot, and after the Battle of Long Island, his home was seized by the British and his family went to Connecticut. The British used his home as a barracks and badly mistreated the house and property. It was not until he returned at the end of the war that he saw the destruction perpetrated on his estate. He had held political positions prior to the Revolutionary War, including as a New York State senator from 1777 to 1783 in the southern region under British control and again after the war from 1784 to 1788. He would go on to other positions later and finally retire to Oneida County, in upstate New York. After the war, he was also promoted to General.[205]

## Chapter 8

# Spies, Patriots and Saboteurs

## Culper Spy Ring

There were different members of the Culper spy ring. Benjamin Tallmadge was the director of military intelligence who created the spy ring operating out of New York City. Robert Townsend was chief informant. Other members were Austin Roe, Caleb Brewster, Abraham Woodhull and Anna Strong.

The Long Island Culper Spy Ring, and spying in general on Long Island during the American Revolution, was a combination of individuals doing extraordinary tasks at a time when getting caught as a spy could mean certain death by hanging or rotting on the horrendous prison ships.

The spy ring that operated on Long Island was of military importance and contributed on more than one occasion to an intervention on behalf of the American army. Since Long Island had constant British troop movements off and on the island and it was a transiting area to Connecticut and New England, there was a continual need for military intelligence information. A lot of information could be obtained informally by someone frequenting the same taverns or parties as British soldiers.

But the route to getting the information to Washington was a circuitous one. Robert Townsend would get the information to Austin Roe, who would get the information to Anna Strong in Setauket, who would signal in which Long Island inlet Abraham Woodhull and Caleb Brewster should meet.

Caleb Brewster would then get the information across the Long Island Sound to Benjamin Tallmadge in Connecticut, who would get the information to George Washington in New Jersey.

## Benjamin Tallmadge

By 1778, Benjamin Tallmadge, whose code name was John Bolton, was head of the spy system on Long Island that reported to General George Washington. Benjamin Tallmadge, born in 1754, was from Suffolk County's Town of Setauket and was the son of a Presbyterian minister. He chose men for this spy system who were familiar to him and whom he could trust. Benjamin Tallmadge oversaw this system for five years while Long Island was occupied and was never caught. General Washington never knew who the people were who worked under Tallmadge in this system.[206]

Tallmadge was part of the Second Regiment, Light Dragoons. He was a Patriot, having been first commissioned as a lieutenant in a Connecticut regiment, much like Nathan Hale. He was in the Battle of Long Island and covered the escape of the troops under the cloak of darkness and providential fog from Brooklyn to New York City. Many battles followed for him, including White Plains, Brandywine and Monmouth. As a result of his service, George Washington appointed him for the important position of heading the spy system on Long Island.[207]

George Washington had written a letter to Major Benjamin Tallmadge on March 21, 1779, in which he related that "hard money" was very difficult to come by. He also gave directions for a less "circuitous route," suggesting Tallmadge send the spy letters through different officers at Elizabethtown or Newark and provide the information that he particularly wanted, such as "arrivals and departures of troops" and "strength and destination of them." He wanted the latest, most up-to-date information in the most direct manner. He finished the letter with a question, asking about the "depth of water" through Hell Gate and the largest ship that had ever passed through it.[208]

Benjamin Tallmadge was an astute officer and deeply involved in helping to win the war effort. He served in many battles, including Harlem Heights, Brandywine and Monmouth. He was honored to have been promoted to captain in December 1776 and to have been chosen for the Dragoons.[209]

In his memoir, in reference to the spy system, he was fairly evasive, stating:

*This year* [1778] *opened a private correspondence with some persons in New York* [for General Washington], *which lasted through the war. How beneficial it was to the Commander-in-Chief is evidenced by his continuing the same to the close of the war. I kept one or more boats continually employed in crossing the Sound on this business.*[210]

# Robert Townsend

Robert Townsend was Benjamin Tallmadge's right-hand man and a major contributor of Revolutionary War espionage information. He was called Samuel Culper Jr. and was from Oyster Bay, Long Island, the son of Samuel Townsend, who owned Raynham Hall. Robert Townsend posed as a Tory merchant and befriended British soldiers in New York City, from whom he obtained valuable information while collecting food luxuries that he might not have obtained elsewhere. He was also considered a society writer for the Rivington newspaper.[211]

Although Rivington was considered a Patriot and publisher of the *Royal Gazette*, his service as a member of the spy ring was in jeopardy because of the perception that he "enriched himself under the mild and wise government of George III." After evacuation, it was demanded that he cease his business in New York City after he was given a public beating. Perceptions, real or imagined, that someone was a Loyalist were grounds for

Townsend Cemetery, Oyster Bay. *Courtesy of the Oyster Bay Historical Society.*

violence after the war.[212] Because of Townsend's society connection, he was widely known in British circles, and his educated manner allowed him access to particular people who unwittingly gave him information that he passed along to the spy network, oftentimes through his coffee shop and general merchandise store in New York City.[213]

Robert Townsend is buried in Oyster Bay.

# Austin Roe

Austin Roe was the messenger for Robert Townsend. Roe owned a store and a tavern. A sign today designates the area where the tavern once stood. He rode the fifty-five miles back and forth through British-held areas without being detected. This he did several times a week. In a typical exchange between Austin Roe and Robert Townsend, Roe brought a clandestine letter from Major Tallmadge to Townsend at his coffee shop near Wall Street. The letter was coded and written in invisible ink. Messages were kept confidential in a variety of ways, including being secreted in a ream of paper.[214]

Austin Roe is buried in Patchogue.

Roe Tavern, Setauket. *Courtesy of Three-Village Historical Society.*

A sign for the tavern of Austin Roe, a member of the Culper spy ring. *Author's photo.*

## ABRAHAM WOODHULL

Abraham Woodhull was named Samuel Culper Sr. in the spy system and was an intricate part of the circuitous route of information. Woodhull's farm in Setauket was his base of operations and where he allowed Austin Roe to pasture his cows so they had a place to hide messages in a secret box.[215]

Abraham Woodhull was a proliferate writer in the spy chain and the recipient of the messages Austin Roe carried from Robert Townsend in New York City. He was responsible for the cattle not getting into enemy hands. The British sent a detachment to seize Woodhull and his men, but Woodhull escaped to Carpenter's Inn and was eventually captured.[216] In one letter of October 31, 1778, Abraham Woodhull indicated how dangerous the work in New York City was and pleaded for the letter's recipient to be careful with the letters lest Woodhull be captured. In another letter of November 20, 1778, he gave details of the British, Yeagers and Dragoon numbers on Long Island. He finished the letter with a hope that his information would be of some help and signed it "Samuel Culper."[217]

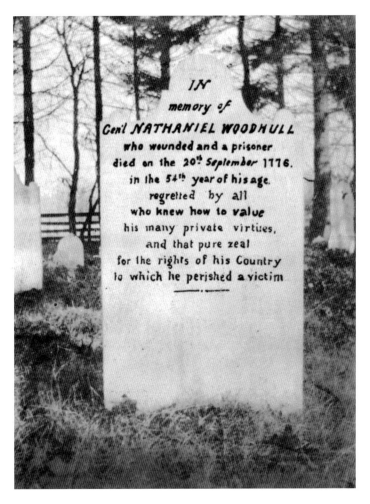

*IN*
*memory of*
*Gen'l NATHANIEL WOODHULL*
who wounded and a prisoner
died on the 20th September 1776.
in the 54th year of his age.
regretted by all
who knew how to value
his many private virtues,
and that pure zeal
for the rights of his Country
to which he perished a victim

The Abraham Woodhull burial site, Setauket. *Courtesy of the Long Island Collection, East Hampton Library.*

## CALEB BREWSTER

Caleb Brewster was fearless and brave. As one of the members of the Culper spy ring, he was the intermediary between Abraham Woodhull's farm in Setauket and Major Tallmadge's headquarters in Connecticut. As a well-known person in Setauket, he was familiar with the inlets and areas and had to keep switching among the six areas to land his boat. As an ex-whaler, he used his whaleboats to cross the Long Island Sound to Connecticut and was responsible for capturing several British supply ships. Anna Smith Strong was the person who informed Abraham Woodhull of Brewster's whereabouts.[218]

Caleb Brewster was a seafarer and familiar with all of the British economic acts that affected seafarers. He, like most of his kind, had anti-British feelings. Brewster's patriotism and actions gained him favor with General Henry Knox. Brewster was then tasked to keep the Long Island Sound clear of the British, for which his familiarity of the coasts and waters prepared him. He served as part of the forces in several missions, including DeLancey's Brigade in Setauket, Fort St. George, Coram and the HMS *Fox*. He was severely wounded in the latter. He would go on in his life to captain a cutter in the US Revenue Service.[219]

## Anna Smith Strong

Anna Smith Strong will be addressed separately in the chapter on women.

## The Spy System

This spy ring operated with efficiency and delicacy. They were a well-working team for almost six years. They operated with a system of code names and simple codes that also involved hanging different articles of wash on a line.

The Culper spy ring cleverly used words and numbers. Originally used by Abraham Woodhull on April 10, 1779, words were taken from *Entick's Dictionary* and written in alphabetical order in columns. Numbers referred to people and areas: New York (10), Setauket (20), Post Riders (30 and 40), General Washington (711), General Clinton (712), Tryon (713), Erskine (714), Vaughn (715), Robinson (716), Brown (717), General Garth (718), Lord North (719), Germain (720), John Bolton (721), Samuel Culper (722), Culper Jr. (723), Austin Roe (724), Caleb Brewster (725) and Rivington (726). Additional numbers were assigned to different places, and an alphabet and numbers were assigned to those places not listed above.[220]

# Nathan Hale

Nathan Hale is one of history's American mysteries because his capture and execution sites are often enigmas. He was supposedly captured on Long Island and executed in New York City, but because there was no official grave, there is a lot of speculation about where these two events occurred.

One source states that "there are three places in New York where our hero was supposedly captured, four where he may have been detained and no less than six where is said to have been hanged."[221]

Nathan Hales's execution is believed to have occurred on September 22, 1776. Some historians state that his execution was on Forty-sixth Street and First Avenue.[222] Others state that it was on Sixty-sixth Street and Third Avenue.

As 1776 approached, Nathan Hale wrote and received many letters to and from family and friends. Several letters to and from his brother Enoch Hale show a concern for family but also a care for daily items needed, the location of his regiment and difficulties encountered by the army.[223]

Henry Onderdonk Jr. writes that two men, Tunis Bogart and Andrew Hegeman, who had been pressed into service by the British to cart ammunition, had witnessed Hale's execution on "an apple tree near Col. Rutgers [farm]." He further states that there were witnesses to the brutality of Cunningham.[224] Hale's execution was additionally a mystery because of what he supposedly said before he was hanged. Many historians will note that he said, "I regret that I have only one life to lose for my country." Yet many people of past generations remember learning that he said, "I regret that I have only one life to give for my country." In either case, his words are very similar to a well-known play of Cato's, from which the words could have been taken.

Another speculation is that Nathan Hale started the horrible New York City fire on September 21, the day before he was hanged. But no proof exists to support this.

After Nathan Hale's death, his brother Enoch bore the news to the family in Coventry, Connecticut. His brother John would later write in the town records, "Capt. Nathan hale, the son of Deacon Richard Hale, was taken in the City of New York by the Britons and Executed as a spy sometime in the month of September, A.D. 1776."[225]

Different accounts have been written as official records by the British, including a letter by a British officer to friends in Britain in which he stated, "Yesterday we hanged an officer of the Provincials who came as a spy."[226]

Nathan Hale's execution. *Courtesy of the Digital Collection, New York Public Library.*

When he was captured, Nathan Hale was in disguise as a schoolteacher, having taught in two different schools in Connecticut. Had he been wearing his army uniform instead of his disguise, he might have become a prisoner of war instead of being hanged as a spy.

Nathan Hale was young, patriotic and selfless. He was well liked and hoped to be of great service to this cause and the beginnings of the new nation. In accepting this position, he had to travel by boat from Connecticut and land on the North Shore of Long Island. Today, a large rock with plaques displaying Hale's words on all four sides is sitting in a prominent spot on an intersection in what is known today as Halesite, near the village of Huntington. Another memorial to him is a larger-than-life statue in City

Nathan Hale rock, Halesite. *Author's photo.*

Hall Park in downtown New York City, near where he was supposedly kept in the Old Gaol (antiquated spelling for jail). Numerous other memorials exist, including a plaque at Sixty-sixth Street and Third Avenue in New York City commemorating his execution.

## Major John Andre

Spying on Long Island was not only relegated to the Patriots. The British, too, had their way of finding out information and trying to foil the plans of their enemy.

Major John Andre, with whom Benedict Arnold conspired to overthrow West Point, was an educated, elite officer in the British army. He had the good fortune to befriend Colonel John Graves Simcoe, who was stationed at Oyster Bay, Long Island, with the Queens Rangers, in proximity to Raynham Hall and Robert Townsend, alias Culper Jr., of the Culper spy ring.

Andre's actions with Benedict Arnold seem to have originated with Arnold, culminating in a letter Arnold, code name John Moore, wrote to

Major Andre, code name John Anderson. The letter detailed the betrayal of West Point into British hands.

Andre was caught near Tarrytown, New York, and executed in Tappan, New York, on October 12, 1780. Some historians state that his execution was in retaliation for the execution of Nathan Hale four years earlier.

# Chapter 9
# Women, Slaves and the War

Women and slaves were both legally marginalized groups before the American Revolution. Slaves, in particular, knew the depths of despair in their situation and the hope of liberty that enveloped the American Revolution.

## WOMEN

The experiences of women during the Revolutionary War generally varied according to their husbands' political affiliation, whether Patriot or Loyalist, and their economic situation in life. Women oftentimes had to maintain the home while husbands were away in the militia or Continental army or at political gatherings, much like future president John Adams's wife, Abigail. Women embargoed British goods, defended homes, changed lifestyles from the use of luxury cloths to cotton homespun, acted as spies and followed husbands, brothers and sweethearts into their encampments to help with cooking, washing, sewing and morale.

The changes in the communities during and after the American Revolution were due in large part to women. There was the patriotic freedom that was engendered by women. "Patriotic mothers nursed the infancy of freedom. Their counsels and their prayers mingled with the deliberations that resulted in a nation's assertion of its independence."[227]

The women of the American Revolution shared in the hardships of the times. Some stood at cannons. Some fought. Some died. They knew that it was the beginnings of a nation that they were helping to forge:

> *We can only dwell upon individual instance of magnanimity, fortitude, self-sacrifice, and heroism, nearing the impress of the feeling of Revolutionary days, indicative of the spirit which animated all, and to which in its various and multiform exhibitions, we are not less indebted to national freedom, than to the swords of the patriots who poured out their blood.*[228]

The American Revolution produced some changes for women, though perhaps not as many as most would have liked. Women still had to wrestle with little political or legal abilities. But gradually throughout the nineteenth century, women would achieve more prominence through writing, education and public support of major causes, like the abolition of slavery. Women would not achieve the right to vote until the Nineteenth Amendment in 1920, and there were many other obstacles that would come about through factory work during industrialization and the ghetto lifestyles of immigrants in New York City and other industrialized cities, particularly on the East Coast.

"The sentiments of the women towards the brave defenders of their native land were expressed in an address widely circulated at the time, and read in the churches of Virginia. 'We know'—it says—'that at a distance from the theatre of war, if we enjoy any tranquility, it is the fruit of your watchings, your labors, your dangers.'"[229] But the American Revolution produced a lot of hope and promise for all types of women. Liberty was not just a catchword of the general but a cry for freedom for all. Eight years of the war showed American fortitude—still evident today—and women were a part of it all.

# Elizabeth Jackson Sands

One woman who was indicative of that gumption was Elizabeth Jackson Sands. Her husband, Colonel John Sands IV (1737–1811), was an officer of the Cow Neck/Great Neck Militia. In August 1776, he and his men fought with General Washington's army to stop the British invasion of New York at the Battle of Long Island on the hills of Brooklyn Heights. After Washington was defeated and the British captured New York, Colonel Sands quickly returned to his farm on Cow Neck. Shortly after his return home, the

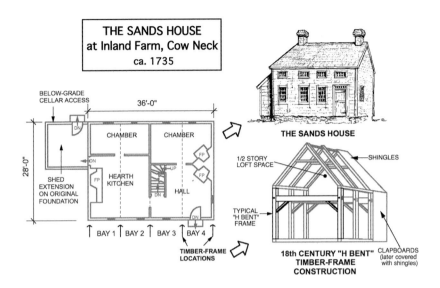

*Above*: The Sands House, 1735. *Courtesy of Fred Blumlein, trustee of the Cow Neck Peninsula Historical Society.*

*Left*: The Sands House, Sands Wing. *Courtesy of Fred Blumlein, trustee of the Cow Neck Peninsula Historical Society.*

British, in their first attempt to arrest him, surrounded his house but failed to apprehend the Colonel. A later attempt by the British succeeded, and he was arrested and imprisoned. He was released on bail and immediately fled across Long Island Sound to rebel-held territory in Connecticut. Subsequently, he sent a message to his wife, Elizabeth Jackson Sands (1735–1806), to gather the kegs of gunpowder hidden on their farm (Inland Farm) and bring it north to Sands Point, where a boat would be waiting at a certain time to ferry it to a wagon. Covered from view and dressed as an old woman, she proceeded to the rendezvous point along with her servant with the intention of returning home after making the delivery. Along the way, they were stopped at a British checkpoint manned by Hessians who arrived on the scene. As the soldiers were about to apprehend them, the two women, realizing the unhappy outcome of their capture, jumped into the boat as it launched and, with the ammunition, successfully joined Colonel Sands in Connecticut.

Women are seldom mentioned as heroes of the Revolution, but the brave story of Elizabeth Jackson Sands and her unnamed servant points to the need to uncover similar stories in order to honor all of the women who sacrificed dearly in the great struggle for our freedom.[230]

# Women of the Revolutionary War

Elizabeth Sands was indicative of many women all over the colonies who contributed in many ways to the American Revolution and, indeed, to the war itself. These women all had similar character traits of strength that gave them the ability to contribute their personal experiences to the foundations of a new nation and to affect other women all over the colonies.

## Mary Washington

Mary Washington was the mother of George Washington and greatly influenced the character of her son. "What she did, and the blessing of a world that follows her—teach impressively—while showing the power—the duty of those who mould the characters of the age to come."[231] She was likened by Lafayette at the time to women of strength of an earlier generation from Rome or Sparta, "fitted to lay the foundation of the greatness of him who towered beyond all Greek—beyond all Roman fame."[232]

Mary Washington saw her son surmount difficulties beyond what she could have imagined. She had engendered in him the qualities developed when she was a younger widow.

## Mercy Otis Warren

At an early age, Mercy Otis was an avid reader, which oftentimes took her away from her household chores. She had a directed reading interest in history through a minister, which would be a great part of her personal education and the foundation for her later writings. Marriage in her mid-twenties to James Warren fueled her personal instruction and connection with political and military figures of the Revolutionary generation, such as Thomas Jefferson, John Adams and Henry Knox.[233] Mercy's quick mind and voracious intellectual thirst gave her the ability to write letters of candor with verses about the Revolutionary era: "The late convulsions are only the natural struggles which ensue when the genius of liberty arises to assert her rights in opposition to the ghost of tyranny."[234] She would go on to write *History of the Rise, Progress and Termination of the American Revolution*, which remains today a respected work of the era.

## Abigail Adams

Abigail Adams can arguably be considered one of the first women's rights advocates as she wrote to her husband, John Adams, during the Continental Congress when the Declaration of Independence was being written: "I desire you would remember the ladies..." The letters between John and Abigail Adams address volumes of Revolutionary fervor. Beginning in 1774, she did not see her husband for long periods before the Revolutionary War, while he was in the Continental Congress, then during and after the war, while he was an ambassador in Europe. Yet she represented the same qualities that women all over the colonies did while their husbands were in politics or in the war. She took care of the farm and provided strength on the homefront while her husband was away. After her husband was out of office, she would write to Mercy Otis Warren, "If we were to count our years by the revolutions we have witnessed, we might number them with the Antediluvians."[235]

## Martha Washington

During the Revolutionary War, Martha Washington's attendance at the winter encampments of her husband and the Continental army were good for the morale of everyone. She was "always welcomed with great joy by the army, and brought a cheering influence which relieved the general gloom in seasons of disaster and despair. Her example was followed by the wives of other general officers."[236] Martha Washington always stayed until the opening of a campaign before she left for Mount Vernon. "She was accustomed afterwards to say that it had been her good fortune to hear the first cannon opening and the last at the closing, of all of the campaigns of the Revolutionary War."[237] She was at the head of the camp followers as she led sewing circles and other morale boosters during encampments. After the war, veterans would go to Mount Vernon to see her in particular.

# Spies

Women became intricately involved in the spying done by Patriots on Long Island during the war. One woman, Anna Smith Strong, known as "Nancy," would be intricately involved in the Culper spy ring.

Anna Smith was born in 1740, the daughter and granddaughter of prominent families who built St. George's Manor on Strong's Neck in Setauket, across the Long Island Sound from Fairfield, Connecticut. Anna's family was Loyalist, but Anna married Judge Strong, a Patriot, and moved to St. George's Manor. When their home was taken by the British, the Strongs moved across Conscience Bay, and Anna became involved as a Patriot spy.

Anna's part in the Culper spy ring, as a housewife and mother, was to use the items of her everyday life—clothes, handkerchiefs and petticoats on a clothesline—as signals to indicate which coves Caleb Brewster's boats were in.

Anna's husband was a Patriot who served in the Suffolk County militia and was imprisoned on the British prison ship *Jersey*. With help from her Tory relations, Anna was able to secure a British pass and bring food and provisions to her husband, which virtually saved his life. She was also able to help get him released.[238]

## Sally Townsend

Sarah Townsend, also known as Sally, was the daughter of Samuel Townsend and sister of Robert Townsend, one of the major figures of the Culper spy ring on Long Island. Some historians speculate about her involvement in the spy ring, and others considered her just an object of flirtation for British officers.

Sally was attractive and the object of attention for many British officers who came to the Townsend family home in Oyster Bay, Raynham Hall. One of these officers was Major John Andre, who would later be in collusion with Benedict Arnold to hand over West Point, the plot that led to Andre's execution. In 1779, on Valentine's Day, Captain John Graves Simcoe read a poem in honor of Sally.[239]

The depth of Sally's intrigue with British officers and what she might have passed along is still to be discovered.

## Agent 355

Robert Townsend, alias Culper Jr., recruited Agent 355, a woman whose name was known only to him. She was invaluable to the Culper spy ring and suffered greatly as a result of her participation.[240]

Agent 355 may possibly have been involved in the passing of information about the Benedict Arnold/John Andre plot to take over West Point, which Arnold eventually learned. Agent 355 was arrested about one month later and imprisoned on the ship *Jersey*, the worst of the worst prison ships. She died about five months later.

## Long Island Women

Many Long Island women of different economic levels participated in the American Revolution in a variety of ways. Some had to verbally and physically combat the British takeover of their homes, livestock and possessions.

Women brought food and provisions to prisoners on the prison ships moored off Long Island. Quaker women, who were often given more liberties, provided this support. Several of these women were given commendations by General Washington after the war.

Deborah Townsend, wife of Jonathan Townsend, a soldier in the war, had to defend her home against British soldiers who came demanding supplies. Like many women, she was alone, defending herself and her home with what she had on hand: a bread shovel. The British officer left, stating, "If this woman is a sample of the wives of our opponents, it is useless to think of subduing them."[241]

Mrs. Hanna Brown, a widow, owned a tavern in Oysterponds when, in the autumn of 1777, armed British soldiers came to her house demanding to be let into the room where she kept the liquor. She rushed to the door and placed herself between them and the alcohol, her livelihood. She belittled, yelled, despised and rejected the insistence of an officer, despite his shoving a musket on either side of her at the door. Her determination, fortitude and language caused the officer to go away grumbling without his intended prize.[242]

Women also embargoed British goods and used locally made products. Three women named Ermina, Leticia and Sabrina met to try their hands at the spinning wheel to make their own garments. This was an example that spread across the New England states and turned out to be a challenge and competition between women.[243] Women were also camp followers as they accompanied husbands and male family members to battlefields and encampments. As support, they sewed, cooked, washed, tended wounds and provided general morale. Some women were also prostitutes and not always allowed or wanted in camp, particularly when disturbances were created.

Life was not always easy for women who were camp followers. Many women did this for lack of other means of financial support. As a result, women joined the fight but remained incognito.[244]

## Slaves

The institution of slavery was introduced into the New Netherland colony, which became New York, in 1629. Right from the beginning, slaves' lot in life was difficult, although the Dutch supposedly treated them more humanely. Once the English took over the colony, the treatment of slaves became harsher, including runaway slave laws. One law stated, "If any Servant or Slave shall run away from their Master or Dame, every Justice of the Peace in this Province is hereby authorized & empowered to grant Hue and Cry after the said Servant or Slave, the Master or Dame having first given in Security for the payment of the Charges that shall thereby attend."[245]

By 1730, the laws were even harsher, including punishment for small offenses. This law was in reaction to a plot in 1712 when several white people were killed and nineteen slaves were tried and executed. As a result of this plot, the laws were more rigorously enforced.[246]

During the Revolutionary War, the institution of slavery became difficult for both the British and the Americans because there was the idea that freedom might be a possibility. It could also happen as a result of the chaos of an area of fighting. By 1794, as a result of the Philadelphia convention, a law was passed that allowed for the "gradual abolition of 'the black curse'" There was a slow decline in New York, with attendant laws, until slavery was fully abolished in 1827.[247]

The institution of slavery on Long Island was not fully documented. As wealth became more prevalent on Long Island, it became more "fashionable" to own at least one slave, such as on the Joseph Lloyd Manor in Lloyd Neck. The slaves on Long Island did not do all of the work as in other areas but were only part of the laborers. Long Island did have large farming communities, but the dependency on this kind of labor was not the same as it was in other areas, particularly the South.[248]

Even though documentation was limited, there were slaves on Long Island. Documentation of the sexes and names of slaves exists for Kings, Queens and Suffolk Counties. Bushwick had twenty-one male slaves and twenty-two female slaves, Brooklyn had forty-three males and twenty-four females, Flatbush had fifty-three males and fifty-five females, Flatlands had seventeen males and eighteen females, Gravesend had seventeen males and seventeen females, New Utrecht had thirty-seven males and thirty females, Hempstead had sixty-eight males and forty-eight females in 1755 and seventeen males and twenty-one females of Negro Indian and mulatto background, Newtown had forty-three males and forty-four females, Oyster Bay had fifty-three males and forty-four females and Huntington had forty-eight males and thirty-six females.[249]

In the New York colony (then state), slavery was as much a part of life as it was in the southern colonies until it was ended in New York in 1827. It took the Emancipation Proclamation as an executive order from President Lincoln in 1863 and the Thirteenth Amendment in 1865 to finally and legally abolish slavery.[250]

Slavery was still in full progress in Onderdonk's account of Suffolk County and Kings County. He states that there was a "$10 Reward. Ran Away, a negro man, Retus, speaks English well and plays on the fiddle, took with him a pair of velvet breeches, fiddle & c. Brook Haven, July 89, '83." And yet, in another instance after the war, he states that "John Benson, a mulatto, who shot Capt. Sol Davis, near Jamaica, was hung at N.Y. for burglary, Friday before Sept. 26, '85."[251]

In Kings County, there was a "5 pound reward. Ran away to city of N.Y. from widow Hendrickie Lott, Flatlands, a black negro man, & c., took 3 coats, 8 shirts, 4 trowsers, 2 pair of square silver buckles."[252] Other runaways included "young negro boys, who ran away from Jeronum Lott and another who approached the Royal Garrison Battalion at Quarters, New Lots."[253]

There were also several accounts of runaways in Queens, and a four-dollar reward was offered for "South," a negro who ran away from Captain Tho's (Thomas) Harriet of Jamaica. "He has on specifically mentioned clothes. He was considered bred to the sea."[254] A $6 reward was offered for "Tom," who "tis thought he will try to go out to some privateer."[255]

There were many different recorded accounts given of people who freed their slaves, most of them between 1806 and 1823, but some as early as 1799 and as late as 1824:

*On the 20 of March, 1806, John Wilson manumits and sets free his negro girl Hannah aged 12 years, at the expiration of 14 years, from the 1ˢᵗ of May next; On the 11ᵗʰ of July 1812, Joseph Fox manumits and sets free his slave, named Phittis Benson, aged about 39 years; On 1ˢᵗ of February 1817, manumits and sets free his negro man slave named Harry, aged about 21 years; On the 21ˢᵗ of September, 1822, Jeremiah Johnson manumits and sets free his colored female slave, aged 26 years.*

All of the accounts mentioned have at least one witness. These and all of the accounts removed the last vestiges of slavery in the city of Brooklyn.[256]

As slavery continued in the United States up until the Civil War began in 1861, there were severe penalties for runaway slaves. A stronger Fugitive Slave Act was added to the Compromise of 1850, with fees for certifying runaways. At times, even those freedmen who could produce papers of manumission were taken as runaways.

Runaways who committed crimes of assault often used the distraction and chaos of the war and occupation of Long Island to effect escape. Some were successful, but others were brought back.

The lives of slaves on Long Island could be no harsher than they were in other colonies. The desire of these runaways, particularly of those fleeing to New York City, was to blend in with a population of free blacks or perhaps to be taken in by empathetic people and hidden or sent on a route up north, much like the later Underground Railroad.

Although the Quakers did not take part in acquiring liberty for the colonies through the Revolutionary War, they did take part in acquiring liberty for slaves:

*Samuel Underhill of New York is "dealt with," by the meeting held at Flushing, 5ᵗʰ of 6ᵗʰ mo., 1765, for importing negroes from Africa. He acknowledges his fault and hopes to conduct himself more agreeably to the Friends as hold negro slaves, to inquire into the circumstances and manner of education of the slaves, and give such advice as the nature of the case requires.*[257]

Many Friends who had slaves freed them. "It was further decided the Friends could 'have no unity' with those who held slaves, and that the meeting would receive no collections from slave-holders."[258]

Military service or support was also a possibility. The British offered slaves their freedom if they joined them and if the British won the war. It seemed reasonable to the British to arm Negroes as accomplices to their treachery. Not only would it provide needed labor, as mentioned, but it would also undermine the Patriot cause by taking away their support and labor. This scenario was particularly of concern in the South, where the slave population was more numerous.[259]

The "Negroes," as they were called, worked as teamsters. They were also employed by the British in the "forage service." Their designation on paper was written as "black."[260] There was an issue, though, with giving former slaves weapons considering their desperation of seeking freedom. And the need for laborers was great, so most were employed in that endeavor, though some were given guns as defense.[261]

The Negroes were given their freedom by a proclamation of Sir Henry Clinton, commander in New York, that gave an open invitation to all Negroes "to desert and take refuge with his army in New York." There were three thousand who took advantage of this British offer and another two thousand who went with the Loyalists into exile.[262] In New York, by 1781, when freedom was given to slaves who had already served three years with the owner's consent, the owner received a land bounty.[263]

The African Burial Ground in lower New York City was unearthed after having been covered over by layers of building and history. The slaves who fought for the British and those who fought as American soldiers "fell in the disastrous battles of Long Island in 1776." During the excavation, the bones and skulls that were discovered were distinctly African remains. Liberty was the goal for both white and black soldiers on the American side, but in death, they were buried separately.[264]

## Jupiter Hammon

Jupiter Hammon was born a slave in 1711 to the Lloyd family of Lloyd Neck, Long Island. Even though he was a slave, Jupiter was a respected "member" of the Lloyd family, often helping Henry Lloyd with his business transactions.

Jupiter is considered the first published black poet, having written a religious piece from 1761 titled "An Evening Prayer," which supported his belief in God.

He was sent to live with Henry's son, Joseph Lloyd, a Patriot of the Revolutionary War. Joseph Lloyd's land was taken by the British, and he and Jupiter went to Connecticut along with many other Patriot refugees.

Joseph Lloyd Manor, Lloyd's Neck. *Author's photo.*

After the Revolutionary War, he continued to write and became a leader in the African community in America, encouraging them in the lack of liberty afforded them after the war. He stayed in the Lloyd family and died in the early 1800s.[265]

## Chapter 10

# The War Is Over

## LONG ISLAND EVACUATION BY THE BRITISH

As the fighting ended in October 1781, the return of the Patriots from Connecticut was inevitable, so the beginning of the Loyalists' departure began in 1782. There were significant numbers of Loyalists who went up to Nova Scotia. Records show that a total of 2,472 left for four different areas of Nova Scotia. Within the next year, 1783, approximately 29,000 departed. Loyalists departed all the way up to Evacuation Day in New York City on November 25, 1783.

The tri-state area of New York, New Jersey and Connecticut witnessed a departure of these people, many of them going to New Brunswick. Loyalists in the southern states generally went to the British West Indies, and some went back to England. Within the ranks of the British military, there were many Loyalists. Their point of view was often that they supported their rightful leader(s), King George III and Parliament, and felt not only kinship with the British people but also rightful allegiance, even though the British eventually lost the war. There was still a great hope among the Loyalists of someday returning to America to recover property, and as the issues that eventually led to the War of 1812 continued even after the Treaty of Paris was signed, there was still the hope that the British government would retake its rightful place over America as victor in the War of 1812.[266]

November 25, 1783, is a date in history that signified the changeover in authority from British to American control in New York City. Graphics and paintings of the day herald the triumphant return of General Washington and his army as the British exited.

*Evacuation Day and Washington's Triumphal Entry*, New York City, November 25, 1783. *Courtesy of Prints and Photographs, Library of Congress.*

On Long Island, the British troops were also withdrawn in 1783 under different timelines for the different counties.

There were preliminary treaties signed on January 20, 1783, between Britain and France and Britain and Spain. This had to be done before the British-American treaty. The provisional treaty was ratified by the American Congress on April 15 and signed by the ambassador in Paris on September 3, 1783, then ratified by Congress on January 14, 1783. Between April and November 1783, there were a lot of other significant changes of great importance. Seven thousand Loyalists left New York because of the pending departure of the British. These Loyalists would flee to Canada, the Caribbean and England. Many of the states already had laws in place that exiled these people from political positions and confiscated property. Between June and November, troops departed for home from the Hudson Valley, where they were encamped waiting for disband orders. In June, a protest by soldiers developed in Philadelphia.[267]

Both the immediate period of the end of the fighting on October 19, 1781, at Yorktown and the wider time periods until the Treaty of Paris on September 3, 1783; the signing of the United States Constitution on September 17, 1787; and the subsequent inauguration of George Washington as the first president on April 30, 1789, were major times of change and rebirth, sometimes with great difficulty, for this brand-new nation.

Long Island mirrored the larger picture of the effects of the war on the domestic population. There were celebrations and also sadness. Everywhere there were physical and emotional scars of the impact of a seven-year-long occupying force. And there was a deep division among citizens who had been on opposite sides of the war, once united as fellow Long Islanders, then divided as Patriots versus Loyalists. One piece of evidence of the deep division was in the finality in 1784 of the political and legal separation of the Town of South Hempstead into the Town of North Hempstead, which was Patriot during the war, and the Town of Hempstead, which was Loyalist or Tory. By 1801, South Hempstead was Hempstead.[268]

> *Possibly a sigh of relief went up when the war was declared over and the farmers were permitted to work their fields in peace, although in view of their losses and in spite of the active part which so many of their best sons took in the conflict in the right side, it seemed like adding to the general misery for the Legislature of New York on May 6, 1784, after the British had retired forever, to impose a fine of 37,000 [pounds] on Long Island "as compensation to the other parts of the state for not having been in condition to take an active part in the war against the enemy."*[269]

As part of the evacuation and exile of Loyalists, there was the incremental departure of British and Hessian troops.

Americans were bitter at the thought of making amends or giving compensation for the loss of Loyalist property and possessions. The Tories had defamed Washington and his compatriots, encouraged desertion and mutiny in the American ranks and joined and wore the uniforms of the king. During the war, farmers were selling food to Lord Howe at high prices while Washington's army was impoverished and hungry. In areas like Philadelphia, New York City and in some homes on Long Island, the British and their Loyalist cohorts were living lives of luxury at the expense of the Patriots. The newly established nation, taken from the British with the surrender at Yorktown and the Treaty of Paris on September 3, 1783, was already deeply in debt, and its ability to compensate Loyalist claims was nearly nonexistent. Washington would call them "detestable parricides!"[270]

In Queens County, after the November 25 evacuation of New York City, the British governor of New York, Sir Guy Carlton, kept parts of the surrounding area of New York City, including Staten Island, New

Utrecht and the area around it on Long Island, to hold the troops until ship transportation could be provided on December 4. The areas of Herricks, Hempstead and lands east were to be released before the other areas. The British and Hessian soldiers were moved toward New York City, and gradual release of the British through Newtown and Bushwick took place. Flushing contained thousands of soldiers before departure. Thoughts were that the British patrolled and then Americans took over.[271]

With the finality of evacuation on November 25 from New York City at midday, the Americans started to strategically reenter the city, led in part by Major General Henry Knox. There was the civilian parade led by George Washington and Governor George Clinton with troops on horseback. The festivities went on for days, and a dinner for George Washington and his officers was held on Evacuation Day at Fraunces Tavern in lower New York City.[272]

Evacuation was not without incidents. There were lawsuits against Loyalists, sabotage of Patriot areas and overall reevaluation of the destruction and malaise caused by seven years of war.

In New York City, the British sabotaged the flagpole at the Battery so that the American flag could not be flown initially. But good American ingenuity prevented long-term destruction, and the American flag flew over the city as an artillery salute was fired.[273]

On Long Island in Queens County, the lawsuits against Loyalists had to wait until after the courts reopened in May 1784. The "peace and order" needed to be preserved on Long Island as British troops evacuated and the authority of Americans was set in place. The political offices were given to the Whigs without interference by the Loyalists. Queens County indicted many Loyalists for acts of thievery during the war, such as stealing a horse, cattle or supplies. There were issues, though, with recovery of damages from Loyalists who were able to acquire high-priced Whig lawyers.[274]

In describing the British occupation the Honorable Silas Wood wrote:

*From 1776–1783 the island was occupied by British troops. They traversed it from one end to the other and were stationed at different places during the war. The whole country within British lines was subject to martial law, the administration of justice was suspended, the army was a sanctuary for crime and robbery and the grossest offenses were atoned by the enlistment. Those who remained at home were harassed and plundered of their property, and the inhabitants were generally subject to the orders, and their property to the disposal, of British officers.[275]*

The British government came to the assistance of the "active" Loyalists by making it financially easy for them to immigrate to Canada. The British government gave great concessions and treated these émigrés, for the most part, like fellow citizens. There was, on the part of the British, a "sympathy for men of common blood, common language, traditions, and institutions, across the seas. On the part of the Patriots they had struggled for a long time to find a voice in the corrupt councils of the English court."[276]

In Suffolk County, "the accounts of people of Huntington for property taken by the British, supported by receipts of British officers, or other evidence amounted to £7249.9.6 and was supposed not to contain one-fourth of what was taken. They were sent to N.Y. to be laid before the Commissioners, but were not attended to."[277]

There was also discontentment among the Continental army officers who were promised at least a half-pay pension when they were discharged. The initial promise in October 1780 led to the Newburgh Conspiracy in March 1783. The officers were disgruntled because of "arrears in pay, unsettled food and clothing accounts" and, finally, the pensions. An anonymous letter was circulated to the officers in the encampment at Newburgh, New York, encouraging strenuous acts against the Continental Congress if their grievances were not addressed. Major John Armstrong, who wrote the letter, had the support of several prominent officers. Although General Washington, who was not included in this letter, called his own meeting of the officers within four days, he wrote an eloquent and direct reply appealing to the officers' long military service and integrity. His letter of reply and humble demeanor diffused what could have been a volatile and detrimental situation as the colonies-turned-states changed hands from British control to the Americans.[278]

Evacuation was about both the present and the future. There was a need to deal with the departing British and Hessians and the damage caused by seven years of occupation, which included vandalism, looting, theft, harassment and murder. And then there was the future to contend with. The states were in severe debt, which was a major contributing factor to the Newburgh Conspiracy and to other events like Shays' Rebellion in Massachusetts. On Long Island, forests were decimated, cattle were driven off, precious family heirlooms were taken and citizens of all types were imprisoned or captured as exchange for enemy prisoners.

There were those people who were either unconcerned with which side won the war or trying to profit from both during the war and after

Map of 1784 United States. *Courtesy of the Missouri History Museum, St. Louis.*

depending on the victor. In these instances, people "were then subject to enemy demands and rebel raids alike."[279]

Other problems concerned property, in the form of both land and Negro slaves. One estimate said that the British had taken back with them approximately three thousand slaves who were worth about $200 each at that time.[280] Loyalists, many owning property, left New York in 1782. One estimate is that twenty-nine thousand Loyalists left New York that year.[281] In New York, the 1779 Confiscation Act "named fifty-nine gentlemen, most of them considerable reputation and property, whose estates were to be forfeited."[282]

On Long Island, "the New York Legislature fined the residents twenty-thousand pounds for lack of enthusiasm for the Patriot cause during the British occupation." And at the end of the war, no tree on Long Island over six inches in circumference was left standing, except the Great Oak in Lloyd Neck. Most fences and orchards were also used as firewood by the British troops in Huntington and New York City.[283]

# The Future

The evacuation also produced seeds of inspiration and hope for the future. Evacuation from New York City and Long Island was not the end of the story. The immediate and long-term effects were both important. On December 4, 1783, George Washington had a meal for his officers at Fraunces Tavern in New York City. His time with them was filled with emotion, as one era was ending and another was beginning. He bid each man to come to him to say goodbye because it was too difficult for him to go to each of them.

The two hereditary laws of Entailing and Primogeniture were being abolished, as is evidenced by two laws passed in Virginia in and around 1785. These laws, the Virginia Act Abolishing Entail on Estates and the Virginia Act on Descent on Estates, Abolishing Primogeniture, would change the way landholdings were handed down in families.[284]

Religious freedom would also become more of a reality, as states pronounced "that man shall be compelled to frequent or support any religious worship, place, or ministry whatsoever."[285] The United States Constitution, adopted on September 17, 1787, would solidify this theme in stating "but no religious test shall ever be required as a Qualification to any office or public trust under the United States."[286]

Slavery was still in effect but being whittled down state by state in the North. Pennsylvania passed the Pennsylvania Act for the Gradual Abolition of Slavery: Statutes at Large of Pennsylvania in 1780, in which it was stated, "It is sufficient to know that all are the work of an Almighty Hand."[287]

Women had hoped for more political and legal rights. Women were weighing their options more in considering marriage or being old maids.[288] Education would become more available to them in the 1800s as more colleges were built and the need for medical and legal professionals expanded.

The Treaty of Paris (1783), which ended the Revolutionary War, would delegate the land given to the United States by the British. The relationship with both the British and the French would be a work in progress for the next few decades.

After the December 4, 1783 meal at Fraunces Tavern, George Washington went to Annapolis, Maryland, to resign his commission to the Continental Congress and then headed home to Mount Vernon with the hope of being a farmer again. Less than six years later, his county would call him again, this time to take the oath of office in New York City in order to serve as the first President of the United States.

*Appendix*

# The Documents

## Huntington Declaration of Rights

*This is the first record in the Huntington Town Clerk's Archives signaling the approach of the Revolution, June 21, 1774.*

1st That every freemans property is absolutely his own, and no man has a right to take it from him without his consent expressed either by himself or his representatives. 2nd That therefore all taxes and duties imposed on His Majestys subjects in the American colonies by the authority of Parliament are wholly unconstitutional and a plain violation of the most essential rights of British subjects. 3rd That the act of Parliament lately passed for shutting up the port of Boston or any other means or device under color of law to compel them or any other of His Majestys American subjects to submit to Parliamentary taxation are subversive to their just and constitutional liberty. 4th That we are of opinion that our brethren of Boston are now suffering in the common cause of British America. 5th That therefore it is the indispensable duty of all colonies to unite in some effectual measures for the repeal of said act, and every other act of Parliament whereby they are taxed for raising a revenue. 6th That it is the opinion of this meeting that the most effectual means for obtaining a speedy repeal of said acts will be to break off all commercial intercourse with Great Britain Ireland and the English West India colonies. 7th And we hereby declare ourselves ready to enter into these or such other measures as shall be agreed upon by a general congress of all the colonies; and we recommend to the general congress to take such measures as shall be more effectual to prevent such goods as are at present in America from being raised to an extravagant price And lastly, we appoint Colonel Platt Conklin, John Sloss Hobart, Esq. and Thomas Wickes a committee for this town, to act in conjunction with the committees of the other towns in the county, as a general committee for the county, to correspond with the committee of New York. Israel Wood President (Courtesy of the Huntington Town Clerk's Archives at Town Hall, online)

# The Continental Association, October 20, 1774

To obtain redress of these grievances, which threaten destruction to the lives, liberty, and property of his majesty's subjects, in North America, we are of opinion, that a non-importation, non-consumption, and non-exportation agreement, faithfully adhered to, will prove the most speedy, effectual, and peaceable measure: and, therefore, we do, for ourselves, and the inhabitants of the several colonies, whom we represent, firmly agree and associate, under the sacred ties of virtue, honour and love of our country, as follows:

1. That from and after the first day of December next, we will not import, into British America, from Great-Britain or Ireland, any goods, wares, or merchandise whatsoever, or from any other place, any such goods, wares, or merchandise, as shall have been exported from Great-Britain or Ireland; nor will we, after that day, import any East-India tea from any part of the world; nor any molasses, syrups, paneles, coffee, or pimento, from the British plantations or from Dominica; nor wines from Madeira, or the Western Islands; nor foreign indigo.

2. We will neither import nor purchase, any slave imported after the first day of December next; after which time, we will wholly discontinue the slave trade, and will neither be concerned in it ourselves, nor will we hire our vessels, nor sell our commodities or manufactures to those who are concerned in it.

3. As a non-consumption agreement, strictly adhered to, will be an effectual security for the observation of the non-importation, we, as above, solemnly agree and associate, that, from this day, we will not purchase or use any tea, imported on account of the East-India company, or any on which a duty hath been or shall be paid; and from and after the first day of March next, we will not purchase or use any East-India tea whatever;

nor will we, nor shall any person for or under us, purchase or use any of those goods, wares, or merchandise, we have agreed not to import, which we shall know, or have cause to suspect, were imported after the first day of December, except such as come under the rules and directions of the tenth article hereafter mentioned.

4. The earnest desire we have, not to injure our fellow-subjects in Great-Britain, Ireland, or the West-Indies, induces us to suspend a non-exportation, until the tenth day of September, 1775; at which time, if the said acts and parts of acts of the British parliament herein after mentioned are not repealed, we will not, directly or indirectly, export any merchandise or commodity whatsoever to Great-Britain, Ireland, or the West-Indies, except rice to Europe.

5. Such as are merchants, and use the British and Irish trade, will give orders, as soon as possible, to their factors, agents and correspondents, in Great-Britain and Ireland, not to ship any goods to them, on any pretence whatsoever, as they cannot be received in America; and if any merchant, residing in Great-Britain or Ireland, shall directly or indirectly ship any goods, wares or merchandise, for America, in order to break the said non-importation agreement, or in any manner contravene the same, on such unworthy conduct being well attested, it ought to be made public; and, on the same being so done, we will not, from thenceforth, have any commercial connexion with such merchant.

6. That such as are owners of vessels will give positive orders to their captains, or masters, not to receive on board their vessels any goods prohibited by the said non-importation agreement, on pain of immediate dismission from their service.

7. We will use our utmost endeavours to improve the breed of sheep, and increase their number to the greatest extent; and to that end, we will kill them as seldom as may be, especially those of the most profitable kind; nor will we export any to the West-Indies or elsewhere; and those of us, who are or may become overstocked with, or can conveniently spare any sheep, will dispose of them to our neighbours, especially to the poorer sort, on moderate terms.

8. We will, in our several stations, encourage frugality, economy, and industry, and promote agriculture, arts and the manufactures of this country, especially that of wool; and will discountenance and discourage every species of extravagance and dissipation, especially all horse-racing, and all kinds of gaming, cock-fighting, exhibitions of shews, plays, and other expensive diversions and entertainments; and on the death of any relation or friend,

none of us, or any of our families, will go into any further mourning-dress, than a black crape or ribbon on the arm or hat, for gentlemen, and a black ribbon and necklace for ladies, and we will discontinue the giving of gloves and scarves at funerals.

9. Such as are venders of goods or merchandise will not take advantage of the scarcity of goods, that may be occasioned by this association, but will sell the same at the rates we have been respectively accustomed to do, for twelve months last past.—And if any vender of goods or merchandise shall sell any such goods on higher terms, or shall, in any manner, or by any device whatsoever violate or depart from this agreement, no person ought, nor will any of us deal with any such person, or his or her factor or agent, at any time thereafter, for any commodity whatever.

10. In case any merchant, trader, or other person, shall import any goods or merchandise, after the first day of December, and before the first day of February next, the same ought forthwith, at the election of the owner, to be either re-shipped or delivered up to the committee of the county or town, wherein they shall be imported, to be stored at the harbor of the importer, until the non-importation agreement shall cease, or be sold under the direction of the committee aforesaid; and in the last-mentioned case, the owner or owners of such goods shall be reimbursed out of the sales, the first cost and charges, the profit, if any, to be applied towards relieving and employing such poor inhabitants of the Town of Boston, as are immediate sufferers by the Boston port-bill; and a particular account of all goods so returned, stored, or sold, to be inserted in the public papers; and if any goods or merchandises shall be imported after the said first day of February, the same ought forthwith to be sent back again, without breaking any of the packages thereof.

11. That a committee be chosen in every county, city, and town, by those who are qualified to vote for representatives in the legislature, whose business it shall be attentively to observe the conduct of all persons touching this association; and when it shall be made to appear, to the satisfaction of a majority of any such committee, that any person within the limits of their appointment has violated this association, that such majority do forthwith cause the truth of the case to be published in the gazette; to the end, that all such foes to the rights of British-America may be publicly known, and universally condemned as the enemies of American liberty; and thenceforth we respectively will break off all dealings with him or her.

12. That the committee of correspondence, in the respective colonies, do frequently inspect the entries of their custom-houses, and inform each other,

from time to time, of the true state thereof, and of every other material circumstance that may occur relative to this association.

13. That all manufactures of this country be sold at reasonable prices, so that no undue advantage be taken of a future scarcity of goods.

14. And we do further agree and resolve, that we will have no trade, commerce, dealings or intercourse whatsoever, with any colony or province, in North-America, which shall not accede to, or which shall hereafter violate this association, but will hold them as unworthy of the rights of freemen, and as inimical to the liberties of their country.

And we do solemnly bind ourselves and our constituents, under the ties aforesaid, to adhere to this association, until such parts of the several acts of parliament passed since the close of the last war, as impose or continue duties on tea, wine, molasses, syrups, paneles, coffee, sugar, pimento, indigo, foreign paper, glass, and painters' colours, imported into America, and extend the powers of the admiral courts beyond their ancient limits, deprive the American subject of trial by jury, authorize the judge's certificate to indemnify the prosecutor from damages, that he might otherwise be liable to from a trial by his peers, require oppressive security from a claimant of ships or goods seized, before he shall be allowed to defend his property, are repealed.—And until that part of the act of the 12 G. 3. Ch. 24, entitled "An act for the better securing his majesty's dock-yards, magazines, ships, ammunition, and stores," by which any persons charged with committing any of the offences therein described, in America, may be tried in any shire or county within the realm, is repealed—and until the four acts, passed the last session of parliament, viz. that for stopping the port and blocking up the harbor of Boston—that for altering the charter and government of the Massachusetts-Bay—and that which is entitled "An act for the better administration of justice, &c."—and that "for extending the limits of Quebec, &c." are repealed. And we recommend it to the provincial conventions, and to the committees in the respective colonies, to establish such farther regulations as they may think proper, for carrying into execution this association.

The foregoing association being determined upon by the Congress, was ordered to be subscribed by the several members thereof; and thereupon, we have hereunto set our respective names accordingly.

In Congress, Philadelphia, October 20, 1774.

(Courtesy of the Library of Congress)

# The Declaration of Independence

## *In Congress, July 4, 1776*

The unanimous Declaration of the thirteen united States of America, When in the Course of human events, it becomes necessary for one people to dissolve the political bands which have connected them with another, and to assume among the powers of the earth, the separate and equal station to which the Laws of Nature and of Nature's God entitle them, a decent respect to the opinions of mankind requires that they should declare the causes which impel them to the separation.

We hold these truths to be self-evident, that all men are created equal, that they are endowed by their Creator with certain unalienable Rights, that among these are Life, Liberty and the pursuit of Happiness.—That to secure these rights, Governments are instituted among Men, deriving their just powers from the consent of the governed,—That whenever any Form of Government becomes destructive of these ends, it is the Right of the People to alter or to abolish it, and to institute new Government, laying its foundation on such principles and organizing its powers in such form, as to them shall seem most likely to effect their Safety and Happiness. Prudence, indeed, will dictate that Governments long established should not be changed for light and transient causes; and accordingly all experience hath shewn, that mankind are more disposed to suffer, while evils are sufferable, than to right themselves by abolishing the forms to which they are accustomed. But when a long train of abuses and usurpations, pursuing invariably the same Object evinces a design to reduce them under absolute Despotism, it is their right, it is their duty, to throw off such Government, and to provide new Guards for their future security.—Such has been the patient sufferance of these Colonies; and such is now the necessity which constrains them to alter their former Systems of Government. The history of the present King of Great Britain is a history of repeated injuries and usurpations, all having in direct object the establishment of an absolute Tyranny over these States. To prove this, let Facts be submitted to a candid world.

He has refused his Assent to Laws, the most wholesome and necessary for the public good.

He has forbidden his Governors to pass Laws of immediate and pressing importance, unless suspended in their operation till his Assent should be obtained; and when so suspended, he has utterly neglected to attend to them.

He has refused to pass other Laws for the accommodation of large districts of people, unless those people would relinquish the right of Representation in the Legislature, a right inestimable to them and formidable to tyrants only.

He has called together legislative bodies at places unusual, uncomfortable, and distant from the depository of their public Records, for the sole purpose of fatiguing them into compliance with his measures.

He has dissolved Representative Houses repeatedly, for opposing with manly firmness his invasions on the rights of the people.

He has refused for a long time, after such dissolutions, to cause others to be elected; whereby the Legislative powers, incapable of Annihilation, have returned to the People at large for their exercise; the State remaining in the mean time exposed to all the dangers of invasion from without, and convulsions within.

He has endeavoured to prevent the population of these States; for that purpose obstructing the Laws for Naturalization of Foreigners; refusing to pass others to encourage their migrations hither, and raising the conditions of new Appropriations of Lands.

He has obstructed the Administration of Justice, by refusing his Assent to Laws for establishing Judiciary powers.

He has made Judges dependent on his Will alone, for the tenure of their offices, and the amount and payment of their salaries.

He has erected a multitude of New Offices, and sent hither swarms of Officers to harass our people, and eat out their substance.

He has kept among us, in times of peace, Standing Armies without the Consent of our legislatures.

He has affected to render the Military independent of and superior to the Civil power.

He has combined with others to subject us to a jurisdiction foreign to our constitution, and unacknowledged by our laws; giving his Assent to their Acts of pretended Legislation:

For Quartering large bodies of armed troops among us:

For protecting them, by a mock Trial, from punishment for any Murders which they should commit on the Inhabitants of these States:

For cutting off our Trade with all parts of the world:

For imposing Taxes on us without our Consent:

For depriving us in many cases, of the benefits of Trial by Jury:

For transporting us beyond Seas to be tried for pretended offences:

For abolishing the free System of English Laws in a neighbouring Province, establishing therein an Arbitrary government, and enlarging its Boundaries so as to render it at once an example and fit instrument for introducing the same absolute rule into these Colonies:

For taking away our Charters, abolishing our most valuable Laws, and altering fundamentally the Forms of our Governments:

For suspending our own Legislatures, and declaring themselves invested with power to legislate for us in all cases whatsoever.

He has abdicated Government here, by declaring us out of his Protection and waging War against us.

He has plundered our seas, ravaged our Coasts, burnt our towns, and destroyed the lives of our people.

He is at this time transporting large Armies of foreign Mercenaries to compleat the works of death, desolation and tyranny, already begun with circumstances of Cruelty & perfidy scarcely paralleled in the most barbarous ages, and totally unworthy the Head of a civilized nation.

He has constrained our fellow Citizens taken Captive on the high Seas to bear Arms against their Country, to become the executioners of their friends and Brethren, or to fall themselves by their Hands.

He has excited domestic insurrections amongst us, and has endeavoured to bring on the inhabitants of our frontiers, the merciless Indian Savages, whose known rule of warfare, is an undistinguished destruction of all ages, sexes and conditions.

In every stage of these Oppressions We have Petitioned for Redress in the most humble terms: Our repeated Petitions have been answered only by repeated injury. A Prince whose character is thus marked by every act which may define a Tyrant, is unfit to be the ruler of a free people.

Nor have We been wanting in attentions to our Brittish brethren. We have warned them from time to time of attempts by their legislature to extend an unwarrantable jurisdiction over us. We have reminded them of the circumstances of our emigration and settlement here. We have appealed to their native justice and magnanimity, and we have conjured them by the ties of our common kindred to disavow these usurpations, which, would inevitably interrupt our connections and correspondence. They too have been deaf to the voice of justice and of consanguinity. We must, therefore, acquiesce in the necessity, which denounces our Separation, and hold them, as we hold the rest of mankind, Enemies in War, in Peace Friends.

We, therefore, the Representatives of the united States of America, in General Congress, Assembled, appealing to the Supreme Judge of the world for the rectitude of our intentions, do, in the Name, and by Authority of the good People of these Colonies, solemnly publish and declare, That these

United Colonies are, and of Right ought to be Free and Independent States; that they are Absolved from all Allegiance to the British Crown, and that all political connection between them and the State of Great Britain, is and ought to be totally dissolved; and that as Free and Independent States, they have full Power to levy War, conclude Peace, contract Alliances, establish Commerce, and to do all other Acts and Things which Independent States may of right do. And for the support of this Declaration, with a firm reliance on the protection of divine Providence, we mutually pledge to each other our Lives, our Fortunes and our sacred Honor.
(Courtesy of the US National Archives and Records Administration)

# ARTICLES OF CONFEDERATION, 1777

To all to whom these Presents shall come, we, the undersigned Delegates of the States affixed to our Names send greeting. Whereas the Delegates of the United States of America in Congress assembled did on the fifteenth day of November in the year of our Lord One Thousand Seven Hundred and Seventy seven, and in the Second Year of the Independence of America agree to certain articles of Confederation and perpetual Union between the States of Newhampshire, Massachusetts-bay, Rhodeisland and Providence Plantations, Connecticut, New York, New Jersey, Pennsylvania, Delaware, Maryland, Virginia, North Carolina, South Carolina, and Georgia in the Words following, viz. "Articles of Confederation and perpetual Union between the States of Newhampshire, Massachusetts-bay, Rhodeisland and Providence Plantations, Connecticut, New York, New Jersey, Pennsylvania, Delaware, Maryland, Virginia, North Carolina, South Carolina, and Georgia.

Article I. The Stile of this confederacy shall be, "The United States of America."

Article II. Each state retains its sovereignty, freedom and independence, and every Power, Jurisdiction and right, which is not by this confederation expressly delegated to the United States, in Congress assembled.

Article III. The said states hereby severally enter into a firm league of friendship with each other, for their common defence, the security of their Liberties, and their mutual and general welfare, binding themselves to assist each other, against all force offered to, or attacks made upon them, or any of them, on account of religion, sovereignty, trade, or any other pretence whatever.

Article IV. The better to secure and perpetuate mutual friendship and intercourse among the people of the different states in this union, the free inhabitants of each of these states, paupers, vagabonds and fugitives from Justice excepted, shall be entitled to all privileges and immunities of free citizens in the several states; and the people of each state shall have free ingress and regress to and from any other state, and shall enjoy therein all the privileges of trade and commerce, subject to the same duties, impositions and restrictions as the inhabitants thereof respectively, provided that such restrictions shall not extend so far as to prevent the removal of property imported into any state, to any other State of which the Owner is an inhabitant; provided also that no imposition, duties or restriction shall be laid by any state, on the property of the united states, or either of them.

If any Person guilty of, or charged with, treason, felony, or other high misdemeanor in any state, shall flee from Justice, and be found in any of the united states, he shall upon demand of the Governor or executive power of the state from which he fled, be delivered up, and removed to the state having jurisdiction of his offence.

Full faith and credit shall be given in each of these states to the records, acts and judicial proceedings of the courts and magistrates of every other state.

Article V. For the more convenient management of the general interests of the united states, delegates shall be annually appointed in such manner as the legislature of each state shall direct, to meet in Congress on the first Monday in November, in every year, with a power reserved to each state to recall its delegates, or any of them, at any time within the year, and to send others in their stead, for the remainder of the Year.

No State shall be represented in Congress by less than two, nor by more than seven Members; and no person shall be capable of being delegate for more than three years, in any term of six years; nor shall any person, being a delegate, be capable of holding any office under the united states, for which he, or another for his benefit receives any salary, fees or emolument of any kind.

Each State shall maintain its own delegates in a meeting of the states, and while they act as members of the committee of the states.

In determining questions in the united states, in Congress assembled, each state shall have one vote.

Freedom of speech and debate in Congress shall not be impeached or questioned in any Court, or place out of Congress, and the members of congress shall be protected in their persons from arrests and imprisonments, during the time of their going to and from, and attendance on congress, except for treason, felony, or breach of the peace.

Article VI. No State, without the Consent of the united States, in congress assembled, shall send any embassy to, or receive any embassy from, or enter into any conferrence, agreement, alliance, or treaty, with any King prince or state; nor shall any person holding any office of profit or trust under the united states, or any of them, accept of any present, emolument, office, or title of any kind whatever, from any king, prince, or foreign state; nor shall the united states, in congress assembled, or any of them, grant any title of nobility.

No two or more states shall enter into any treaty, confederation, or alliance whatever between them, without the consent of the united states, in congress assembled, specifying accurately the purposes for which the same is to be entered into, and how long it shall continue.

No State shall lay any imposts or duties, which may interfere with any stipulations in treaties, entered into by the united States in congress assembled, with any king, prince, or State, in pursuance of any treaties already proposed by congress, to the courts of France and Spain.

No vessels of war shall be kept up in time of peace, by any state, except such number only, as shall be deemed necessary by the united states, in congress assembled, for the defence of such state, or its trade; nor shall any body of forces be kept up, by any state, in time of peace, except such number only as, in the judgment of the united states, in congress assembled, shall be deemed requisite to garrison the forts necessary for the defence of such state; but every state shall always keep up a well regulated and disciplined militia, sufficiently armed and accounted, and shall provide and constantly have ready for use, in public stores, a due number of field pieces and tents, and a proper quantity of arms, ammunition, and camp equipage.

No State shall engage in any war without the consent of the united States in congress assembled, unless such State be actually invaded by enemies, or shall have received certain advice of a resolution being formed by some nation of Indians to invade such State, and the danger is so imminent as not to admit of a delay till the united states in congress assembled, can be consulted: nor shall any state grant commissions to any ships or vessels of war, nor letters of marque or reprisal, except it be after a declaration of war by the united states in congress assembled, and then only against the kingdom or State, and the subjects thereof, against which war has been so declared, and under such regulations as shall be established by the united states in congress assembled, unless such state be infested by pirates, in which case vessels of war may be fitted out for that occasion, and kept so long as the danger shall continue, or until the united states in congress assembled shall determine otherwise.

Article VII. When land forces are raised by any state, for the common defence, all officers of or under the rank of colonel, shall be appointed by the legislature of each state respectively by whom such forces shall be raised, or in such manner as such state shall direct, and all vacancies shall be filled up by the state which first made appointment.

Article VIII. All charges of war, and all other expenses that shall be incurred for the common defence or general welfare, and allowed by the united states in congress assembled, shall be defrayed out of a common treasury, which shall be supplied by the several states, in proportion to the value of all land within each state, granted to or surveyed for any Person, as such land and the buildings and improvements thereon shall be estimated, according to such mode as the united states, in congress assembled, shall, from time to time, direct and appoint. The taxes for paying that proportion shall be laid and levied by the authority and direction of the legislatures of the several states within the time agreed upon by the united states in congress assembled.

Article IX. The united states, in congress assembled, shall have the sole and exclusive right and power of determining on peace and war, except in the cases mentioned in the sixth article—of sending and receiving ambassadors—entering into treaties and alliances, provided that no treaty of commerce shall be made, whereby the legislative power of the respective states shall be restrained from imposing such imposts and duties on foreigners, as their own people are subjected to, or from prohibiting the exportation or importation of any species of goods or commodities whatsoever—of establishing rules for deciding, in all cases, what captures on land or water shall be legal, and in what manner prizes taken by land or naval forces in the service of the united Sates, shall be divided or appropriated—of granting letters of marque and reprisal in times of peace—appointing courts for the trial of piracies and felonies committed on the high seas; and establishing courts; for receiving and determining finally appeals in all cases of captures; provided that no member of congress shall be appointed a judge of any of the said courts.

The united states, in congress assembled, shall also be the last resort on appeal, in all disputes and differences now subsisting, or that hereafter may arise between two or more states concerning boundary, jurisdiction, or any other cause whatever; which authority shall always be exercised in the manner following. Whenever the legislative or executive authority, or lawful agent of any state in controversy with another, shall present a petition to congress, stating the matter in question, and praying for a hearing, notice thereof shall be given, by order of congress, to the legislative or executive authority of the other state in controversy, and a day assigned for the appearance of the parties by their lawful agents, who shall then be directed to appoint, by joint consent, commissioners or judges to constitute a court for hearing and determining the matter in question: but if they cannot agree, congress shall name three persons out of each of the united states, and from the list of such persons each party shall alternately strike out one, the petitioners beginning, until the number shall be reduced to thirteen; and from that number not less than seven, nor more than nine names, as congress shall direct, shall, in the presence of congress, be drawn out by lot, and the persons whose names shall be so drawn, or any five of them, shall be commissioners or judges, to hear and finally determine the controversy, so always as a major part of the judges, who shall hear the cause, shall agree in the determination: and if either party shall neglect to attend at the day appointed, without showing reasons which congress shall judge sufficient, or being present, shall refuse to strike, the congress shall proceed to nominate three persons out of each State, and the secretary of congress shall strike in behalf of such party absent or refusing; and the judgment and sentence of the court, to be appointed in the manner before prescribed, shall be final and conclusive; and if any of the parties shall refuse to submit to the authority of such court, or to appear or defend their claim or cause, the court shall nevertheless proceed to pronounce sentence, or judgment, which shall in like manner be final and decisive; the judgment or sentence and other proceedings being in either case transmitted to congress, and lodged among the acts of congress, for the security of the parties concerned: provided that every commissioner, before he sits in judgment, shall take an oath to be administered by one of the judges of the supreme or superior court of the State where the cause shall be tried, "well and truly to hear and determine the matter in question, according to the best of his judgment, without favour, affection, or hope of reward: "provided, also, that no State shall be deprived of territory for the benefit of the united states.

All controversies concerning the private right of soil claimed under different grants of two or more states, whose jurisdictions as they may respect such lands, and the states which passed such grants are adjusted, the said grants or either of them being at the same time claimed to have originated antecedent to such settlement of jurisdiction, shall, on the petition of either party to the congress of the united states, be finally determined, as near as may be, in the same manner as is before prescribed for deciding disputes respecting territorial jurisdiction between different states.

The united states, in congress assembled, shall also have the sole and exclusive right and power of regulating the alloy and value of coin struck by their own authority, or by that of the respective states—fixing the standard of weights and measures throughout the united states—regulating the trade and managing all affairs with the Indians, not members of any of the states; provided that the legislative right of any state, within its own limits, be not infringed or violated—establishing and regulating post-offices from one state to another, throughout all the united states, and exacting such postage on the papers passing through the same, as may be requisite to defray the expenses of the said office—appointing all officers of the land forces in the service of the united States, excepting regimental officers—appointing all the officers of the naval forces, and commissioning all officers whatever in the service of the united states; making rules for the government and regulation of the said land and naval forces, and directing their operations.

The united States, in congress assembled, shall have authority to appoint a committee, to sit in the recess of congress, to be denominated, "A Committee of the States," and to consist of one delegate from each State; and to appoint such other committees and civil officers as may be necessary for managing the general affairs of the united states under their direction—to appoint one of their number to preside; provided that no person be allowed to serve in the office of president more than one year in any term of three years; to ascertain the necessary sums of money to be raised for the service of the united states, and to appropriate and apply the same for defraying the public expenses; to borrow money or emit bills on the credit of the united states, transmitting every half year to the respective states an account of the sums of money so borrowed or emitted,—to build and equip a navy—to agree upon the number of land forces, and to make requisitions from each state for its quota, in proportion to the number of white inhabitants in such state, which requisition shall be binding; and thereupon the legislature of each state shall appoint the regimental officers, raise the men, and clothe, arm, and equip them, in a soldier-like manner, at the expense of the united states; and the officers and men so clothed, armed, and equipped, shall march to the place appointed, and within the time agreed on by the united states, in congress assembled; but if the united states, in congress assembled, shall, on consideration of circumstances, judge proper that any state should not raise men, or should raise a smaller number than its quota, and that any other state should raise a greater number of men than the quota thereof, such extra number shall be raised, officered, clothed, armed, and equipped in the same manner as the quota of such state, unless the legislature of such state shall judge that such extra number cannot be safely spared out of the same, in which case they shall raise, officer, clothe, arm, and equip, as many of such extra number as they judge can be safely spared. And the officers and men so clothed, armed, and equipped, shall march to the place appointed, and within the time agreed on by the united states in congress assembled.

The united states, in congress assembled, shall never engage in a war, nor grant letters of marque and reprisal in time of peace, nor enter into any treaties or alliances, nor coin money, nor regulate the value thereof nor ascertain the sums and expenses necessary for the defence and welfare of the united states, or any of them, nor emit bills, nor borrow money on the credit of the united states, nor appropriate money, nor agree upon the number of vessels of war to be built or purchased, or the number of land or sea forces to be raised, nor appoint a commander in chief of the army or navy, unless nine states assent to the same, nor shall a question on any other point, except for adjourning from day to day, be determined, unless by the votes of a majority of the united states in congress assembled.

The congress of the united states shall have power to adjourn to any time within the year, and to any place within the united states, so that no period of adjournment be for a longer duration than the space of six Months, and shall publish the Journal of their proceedings monthly, except such parts thereof relating to treaties, alliances, or military operations, as in their judgment require secrecy; and the yeas and nays of the delegates of each State, on any question, shall be entered on the Journal, when it is desired by any delegate; and the delegates of a State, or any of them, at his or their request, shall be furnished with a transcript of the said Journal, except such parts as are above excepted, to lay before the legislatures of the several states.

Article X. The committee of the states, or any nine of them, shall be authorized to execute, in the recess of congress, such of the powers of congress as the united states, in congress assembled, by the consent of nine states, shall, from time to time, think expedient to vest them with; provided that no power be delegated to the said committee, for the exercise of which, by the articles of confederation, the voice of nine states, in the congress of the united states assembled, is requisite.

Article XI. Canada acceding to this confederation, and joining in the measures of the united states, shall be admitted into, and entitled to all the advantages of this union: but no other colony shall be admitted into the same, unless such admission be agreed to by nine states.

Article XII. All bills of credit emitted, monies borrowed, and debts contracted by or under the authority of congress, before the assembling of the united states, in pursuance of the present confederation, shall be deemed and considered as a charge against the united states, for payment and satisfaction whereof the said united states and the public faith are hereby solemnly pledged.

Article XIII. Every State shall abide by the determinations of the united states, in congress assembled, on all questions which by this confederation are submitted to them. And the Articles of this confederation shall be inviolably observed by every state, and the union shall be perpetual; nor shall any alteration at any time hereafter be made in any of them, unless such alteration be agreed to in a congress of the united states, and be afterwards con-firmed by the legislatures of every state.

And Whereas it hath pleased the Great Governor of the World to incline the hearts of the legislatures we respectively represent in congress, to approve of, and to authorize us to ratify the said articles of confederation and perpetual union, Know Ye, that we, the undersigned delegates, by virtue of the power and authority to us given for that purpose, do, by these presents, in the name and in behalf of our respective constituents, fully and entirely ratify and confirm each and every of the said articles of confederation and perpetual union, and all and singular the matters and things therein contained. And we do further solemnly plight and engage the faith of our respective constituents, that they shall abide by the determinations of the united states in congress assembled, on all questions, which by the said confederation are submitted to them. And that the articles thereof shall be inviolably observed by the states we respectively represent, and that the union shall be perpetual. In Witness whereof, we have hereunto set our hands, in Congress. Done at Philadelphia, in the State of Pennsylvania, the ninth Day of July, in the Year of our Lord one Thousand seven Hundred and Seventy eight, and in the third year of the Independence of America.

(Courtesy of US National Archives and Records Administration)

# Notes

## INTRODUCTION

1. Ellet, *Women of the American Revolution*, 15.

## CHAPTER 1

2. Luke and Venables, *Long Island in the American Revolution*, 27.
3. Schecter, *Battle for New York*, 5.
4. Smits, "Creating a New County," 129.
5. Ross, *History of Long Island*, 221.
6. Meyer, *Irony of Submission*, 1.
7. Bailyn, *Ideological Origins*, 95.
8. Muzzy, *American History*, 108–09.
9. Ibid., 113.
10. Ibid., 115.
11. Ibid., 117.
12. Ibid., 121.
13. *American Revolution in New York*, 9.
14. Ibid., 11.
15. Naylor, *Roots and Heritage*, 109.
16. Darlington, *Glimpses of Nassau*, 5.
17. O'Shea, *History of North Hempstead*, 5.

## Chapter 2

18. Mollo and McGregor, *Uniforms of the American Revolution*, 33.
19. Ibid., 34.
20. Ibid., 35.
21. Bessell, *Brief History*, 1991, 4.
22. Brown, *King's Friends*, 78.
23. Reynolds, *Long Island*, 27.
24. Mather, *Refugees of 1776*, 88.
25. *American Revolution in New York*, 212–13.
26. Morris, *Encyclopedia of American History*, 90.
27. Smits, "Creating a New County," 129.
28. Bliven, *Battle for Manhattan*, 10.
29. Ibid., 14.
30. Ross, *History of Long Island*, 221.
31. Hibbard, *Rock Hall*.
32. Smits, *Creation of Nassau County*, 4.
33. Allen, *Tories*, 180.
34. Ibid.
35. Mather, *Refugees of 1776*, 145.
36. O'Shea, *History of North Hempstead*, 6.
37. Ross, *History of Long Island*, 219.
38. Ibid., 220.
39. Wilson, *Historic Long Island*, 144–45.

## Chapter 3

40. Wilson, *Historic Long Island*, 144.
41. Lengel, *Glorious Struggle*, 63.
42. Luke and Venables, *Long Island in the American Revolution*, 23.
43. Ibid., 27.
44. Naylor, *Roots and Heritage*, 110.
45. Mather, *Refugees of 1776*, 42, 44, 46.
46. Greene, *Revolutionary*, 35.
47. Ibid., 36.
48. Ibid., 37–39.
49. Fiske, *Washington and His Country*, 214.
50. Mather, *Refugees of 1776*, 48–49.

51. Ibid., 50.
52. Baurmeister, *Revolution in America*, 38–39.
53. Morris, *Encyclopedia of American History*, 93.
54. Fiske, *Washington and His Country*, 215.
55. Ibid., 216.
56. Bunce and Harmond, *Long Island as America*, 75.
57. Ibid., 75.
58. Ibid., 76.
59. Muzzy, *American History*, 136.
60. Coffin, *Boys of '76*, 107.
61. Ross, *History of Long Island*, 215.
62. Coffin, *Boys of '76*, 108.
63. Ross, *History of Long Island*, 215.
64. Ibid., 219.
65. Bunce and Harmond, *Long Island as America*, 79.
66. Ibid., 80.
67. Ibid., 81.
68. Armbruster, *Wallabout Prison Ships*, 14–16.
69. Ibid., 17–21.
70. Onderdonk, *Revolutionary Incidents*, 172.
71. Jones, *History of New York*, 115.
72. Onderdonk, *Revolutionary Incidents*, 167.
73. Ibid., 171.

## Chapter 4

74. Overton, *Long Island's Story*.
75. Smits, *Creation of Nassau*, 129.
76. O'Shea, *History of North Hempstead*.
77. Smits, *Creation of Nassau County*, 6.
78. Ibid., 7.
79. Ibid., 8.
80. O'Shea, *History of North Hempstead*, 7.
81. Onderdonk, *Documents and Letters*, 43–44.
82. Ibid., 52.
83. Ibid., 54.
84. Mather, *Refugees of 1776*, 145.

85. Ibid., 146.
86. Onderdonk, *Documents and Letters*, 168.
87. Riker, *Annals of Newtown*, 183.
88. Ibid., 185.
89. Ibid., 188.
90. Mather, *Refugees of 1776*, 167.
91. Schneider, "British Occupancy of Flushing," 232.
92. Waller, *History of Flushing*, 134.
93. "Flushing's Revolutionary History."
94. Waller, *History of Flushing*, 135.
95. Ibid., 135.
96. Schneider, "British Occupancy of Flushing," 232.
97. Waller, *History of Flushing*, 136–39.
98. Ibid., 140–42.
99. Onderdonk, *Documents and Letters*, 35.
100. Brush, "Long Island's Heroes of '76," 8.
101. Wettingfeld, "Queens Tories Captured."
102. Kiernan and D'Agnese, *Signing Their Lives Away*, 76–77.
103. Onderdonk, *Documents and Letters*.
104. Ibid., 74.
105. Ibid., 172–73.
106. Ibid., 24–25.
107. Schultz, *Colonial Hempstead*, 279.
108. Naylor, *Roots and Heritage*, 109–10.
109. Schultz, *Colonial Hempstead*, 263.
110. *Queen's Rangers*.
111. Van Santvoord, "Revolutionary Incidents."

## Chapter 5

112. Onderdonk, *Revolutionary Incidents*, 13.
113. Ibid., 27.
114. Ibid., 75.
115. Ibid., 30.
116. Bayles, *Early Years*, 21.
117. Mather, *Refugees of 1776*, 220.
118. Ibid., 222.
119. Ibid., 223.

120. Ibid., 224.
121. Onderdonk, *Revolutionary Incidents*, 107.
122. Bayles, *Early Years*, 23.
123. Vincitorio, "Revolutionary War," 69.
124. *Meigs Battle of Sag Harbor*.
125. Bayles, *Early Years*, 25.
126. Luke and Venables, *Long Island in the American Revolution*, 49.
127. East Hampton Library Document Book, vol. 1, n.d., 43.
128. Luke and Venables, *Long Island in the American Revolution*, 50.
129. Bayles, *Early Years*, 25.
130. Ibid.
131. Mather, *Refugees of 1776*, 88.
132. Ibid., 88.
133. Bayles, *During the Revolution*, 6.
134. Bayles, "Capture of General Woodhull."
135. Maxwell, *Portrait of William Floyd*, 17–20.
136. Bayles, *During the Revolution*, 6.
137. Bayles, *Early Years*.

# CHAPTER 6

138. Onderdonk, *Documents and Letters*, 32.
139. Ibid., *Revolutionary Incidents*, 7.
140. Mather, *Refugees of 1776*, 149.
141. Ibid., 148–50.
142. Thompson, *History of Long Island*, 282.
143. Ibid., 286.
144. Bailyn, *Ideological Origins*, 95–96.
145. Ross, *History of Long Island*, 146.
146. Ibid., 62.
147. Rines, *Old Historic Churches*, 146–47.
148. Disoway, *Earliest Churches of New York*, 323.
149. Onderdonk, *Revolutionary Incidents*, 172.
150. Rines, *Old Historic Churches*, 136.
151. Bayles, *Early Years*, 11–12.
152. Ibid., 13.
153. Bayles, *Middle Island Presbyterian Church*, 2.
154. Disoway, *Earliest Churches of New York*, 300.

155. Onderdonk, *Revolutionary Incidents*, 82–83.
156. Disoway, *Earliest Churches of New York*.
157. Ibid., 291–301.
158. *Long Island Press*, "Jamaica."
159. Moore, *History of St. George's Church*, 123.
160. Ibid., 124–25.
161. Ladd, *Origin and History of Grace Church*, 94.
162. Ibid., 96–97.
163. Waller, *History of Flushing*, 130, 132–33.
164. Eberlein, *Manor Houses and Historic Homes*, 25–26.
165. Ross, *History of Long Island*, 163.
166. "History of Manhasset Meeting."

## Chapter 7

167. Chitwood, *History of Colonial America*, 528.
168. Schlesinger, *Colonial Merchants*, 423–24.
169. Chitwood, *History of Colonial America*, 647.
170. Ibid., 647.
171. Ibid., 636.
172. Schlesinger, *Colonial Merchants*, 450.
173. Ibid., 425.
174. Maxwell, *Portrait of William Floyd*, 21.
175. Waller, *History of Flushing*, 146.
176. Radune, *Sound Rising*, 4.
177. Onderdonk, *Revolutionary Incidents*, 7.
178. Luke and Venables, *Long Island in the American Revolution*, 19–21.
179. Maxwell, *Portrait of William Floyd*, 24.
180. Onderdonk, *Documents and Letters*, 175.
181. Vincitorio, "Revolutionary War," 70.
182. Ibid., 77–78.
183. Luke and Venables, *Long Island in the American Revolution*, 37.
184. Ibid., 38.
185. Jones, *History of New York*, 262.
186. Wanzor, *Patriots of the North Shore*, 26.
187. Ibid., 27.
188. Naylor, *Roots and Heritage*, 113.
189. Bessell, *Brief History of Huntington*.

190. Folprecht, "When Redcoats Ruled."
191. "Economic Consequences."
192. Ross, *History of Long Island*, 222.
193. Kuehas, "Reluctant Host," 7.
194. Mather, *Refugees of 1776*, 200.
195. Ibid., 201.
196. Ibid., 207.
197. Ibid., Ap. D, #28, 881.
198. Ibid., #39, 883.
199. Ibid., 210.
200. Ibid., 212.
201. Ibid., 216.
202. Kuehas, "Reluctant Host," 1, 4, 8.
203. Eberlein, *Manor Houses and Historic Homes*, 148, 150–52.
204. Ibid., 132–33.
205. Ibid., 111–12.

# Chapter 8

206. Bayles, *During the Revolution*.
207. Reynolds, *Long Island*.
208. Lengel, *Glorious Struggle*.
209. Tallmadge, *Memoir*.
210. Ibid., 29.
211. Manley, *Long Island Discovery*, 81.
212. Spaulding, *New York in the Critical Period*, 125–26.
213. Bayles, *During the Revolution*, 11.
214. Ibid., 11–12.
215. Ibid., 11.
216. Onderdonk, *Documents and Letters*, 89.
217. Pennypacker, *General Washington's Spies*, 32, 35.
218. Bayles, *During the Revolution*, 12.
219. Reynolds, *Long Island*, 36.
220. Pennypacker, *General Washington's Spies*, 209–10.
221. Kirby, "Nathan Hale Was Here," 3.
222. Alper, *America's Freedom Trail*, 230.
223. Seymour, *Documentary Life*, 79–80, 83–84.
224. Onderdonk, *Documents and Letters*, 204.

225. Pennypacker, *General Washington's Spies*, 20.
226. Ibid., 21.

## Chapter 9

227. Ellet, *Women of the American Revolution*, 14.
228. Ibid., 15.
229. Ibid., 19.
230. Blumlein, *Elizabeth Sands*.
231. Ellet, *Women of the American Revolution*, 24.
232. Ibid., 228.
233. Ibid., 74–76.
234. Ibid., 83.
235. Ibid., 30.
236. Ibid., 12.
237. Ibid., 13.
238. Currie, *Anna Smith Strong*, 9, 11–13.
239. Reynolds, *Long Island*, 22.
240. DePauw, *Four Traditions*, 32.
241. Van Santvoord, "Revolutionary Incidents," 24–25.
242. Naylor, *Roots and Heritage*, 36.
243. DePauw, *Four Traditions*, 15.
244. Norton, *Liberty's Daughters*, 212–13.
245. Ross, *History of Long Island*, 119.
246. Ibid., 220.
247. Ibid., 121.
248. Ibid.
249. Ibid., 121–28.
250. Fish, *Battleground*, 235.
251. Onderdonk, *Revolutionary Incidents*, 109.
252. Ibid., 185.
253. Ibid., 199.
254. Ibid., 157.
255. Ibid., 163.
256. Ross, *History of Long Island*, 130–32.
257. Waller, *History of Flushing*, 152.
258. Ibid., 153.
259. Quarles, *Negro in the American Revolution*, 112.

260. Ibid., 134–35.
261. Ibid., 146.
262. Fish, *Battleground*.
263. Ibid., 237.
264. Nell, *Colored Patriots*, 151.
265. "Jupiter Hammon."

## Chapter 10

266. Mather, *Refugees of 1776*, 147–48.
267. Morris, *Encyclopedia of American History*, 110.
268. Naylor, *Roots and Heritage*.
269. Ross, *History of Long Island*, 221.
270. Muzzy, *American History*, 153.
271. Onderdonk, *Revolutionary Incidents*, 252–53.
272. *Toast to Freedom*, 8.
273. Ibid., 266.
274. Onderdonk, *Documents and Letters*, 258–59.
275. Ross, *History of Long Island*, 221–22.
276. Muzzy, *American History*, 155.
277. Onderdonk, *Revolutionary Incidents*, 110.
278. Morris, *Encyclopedia of American History*, 109–10.
279. Meyer, *Irony of Submission*, 35.
280. Spaulding, *New York in the Critical Period*, 117.
281. Ibid., 123.
282. Ibid., 121.
283. Meyer, *Irony of Submission*, 37.
284. Pole, *Revolution in America*, 545–47.
285. Ibid., 550.
286. United States Constitution (1787).
287. Pole, *Revolution in America*, 551.
288. Norton, *Liberty's Daughters*, 241.

# Bibliography

Allen, Thomas B. *Tories: Fighting for the King in America's First Civil War*. New York: Harper Collins Publishers, 2010.

Alper, Victor. *America's Freedom Trail: Massachusetts, New York, New Jersey, Pennsylvania*. New York: MacMillan, 1976.

*The American Revolution in New York: Its Political, Social, and Economic Significance*. Division of Archives and History. New York: University of the State of New York, 1926.

Armbruster, Eugene L. *The Wallabout Prison Ships, 1776–1783*. New York, 1920.

Bailyn, Bernard. *The Ideological Origins of the American Revolution*. Cambridge, MA: Harvard University Press, 1992.

Baurmeister, Carl Leopold. *Revolution in America: Confidential Letters and Journals, 1776–1784, of Adjutant General Major Baurmeister of the Hessian Forces*. Westport, CT: Greenwood Press, 1973.

Bayles, Thomas R. "Capture of General Nathaniel Woodhull." *Long Island Forum* (December 1947).

———. *During the Revolution in Brookhaven Town*. Brookhaven, NY: Brookhaven Town Bicentennial Commission, n.d.

———. *The Early Years in Brookhaven Town*. Middle Island, NY, 1962.

———. *History of the Middle Island Presbyterian Church, 1766–1970*. N.p., n.d.

Beeman, Richard R. *Our Lives, Our Fortunes, and Our Sacred Honor: The Forging of American Independence, 1774–1776*. New York: Basic Books, 2013.

Bessell, Matthew. *A Brief History of the Town of Huntington*. Huntington, NY: Town Historian, 1991.

———. *A Brief History of the Town of Huntington*. 7th printing. Huntington, NY: Office of Historian, 1994.

Bliven, Bruce, Jr. *Battle for Manhattan*. New York: Henry Holt and Company, 1956.

Blumlein, Fred. *Elizabeth Sands*. N.p., September 2015.

Brown, Wallace. *The King's Friends: The Composition and Motives of the American Loyalists Claimants*. Providence, RI: Brown University Press, n.d.

Brush, Hale. "Long Island's Heroes of '76." *Long Island Life* (September 1926).

Bunce, James, and Richard P. Harmond. *Long Island as America: A Documentary History to 1896*. Port Washington, NY: Kennikat Press, 1977.

Chitwood, Oliver Perry. *A History of Colonial America*. New York: Harper & Brothers, 1948.

Coffin, Charles Carleton. *The Boys of '76: A History of the Battles of the Revolution*. New York: Harper & Brothers, 1904.

"Culper Spy Ring." www.mountvernon.org/research-collections/digital-encyclopedia/article/culper-spy-ring.

Currie, Catheriune. *Anna Smith Strong and the Setauket Spy Ring*. N.p., n.d.

Darlington, Oscar. *Glimpses of Nassau County's History.* Mineola, NY: Nassau County Trust Company, 1949.

DePauw, Linda Grant. *Four Traditions: Women of New York During the American Revolution.* New York: New York State American Revolution Bicentennial Commission, 1974.

Disoway, Gabriel. *The Earliest Churches of New York and Its Vicinity.* N.p.: Library of Oxford University, 1865. https://www.archive.org/details/earliestchurche00disogoog.

*East Hampton Library Document Book.* Vol. 1, p. 43.

Eberlein, Harold Donaldson. *Manor Houses and Historic Homes of Long Island and Staten Island.* Port Washington, NY: Ira J. Friedman, Inc., 1966.

"Economic Consequences." http://ushistory.org/us/11e.asp.

Ellet, Elizabeth. *The Women of the American Revolution.* 2 vols. New York: Baker and Scribner, 1848.

*Encyclopedia of American History,* s.v. "British Evacuate Boston." New York: Harper & Brothers, 1953.

Fish, Hamilton. *The Battleground of the Revolutionary War.* New York: Vantage Press, 1976.

Fiske, John. *Washington and His Country.* Boston: Ginn & Company, 1889.

*Flushing Journal.* "Flushing's Revolutionary History." August 6, 1864.

Folprecht, William. "When Redcoats Ruled Long Island." *Newsday,* October 9, 1965.

Greene, Francis Vinton. *The Revolutionary War and the Military Policy of the United States.* New York: Charles Scribner's Sons, 1911.

Griffin, Augustus. "Heroism on Occupied Long Island, 1776–1783." In *Journeys on Old Long Island: Travelers' Accounts, Contemporary Descriptions, and*

*Residents Reminiscences, 1744–1893*, edited by Natalie Naylor. Interlaken, NY: Empire State Books, 2002.

Hibbard, Shirley G. *Rock Hall: A Narrative History*. Mineola, NY: Friends of Rock Hall, Dover Publications, 1997.

"History of Manhasset Meeting." https://www.nyym.org/manhasset/history.html.

Jones, Thomas. *History of New York During the Revolutionary War*. Vol. 1. New York: Arno Press for the New York Historical Society, 1879.

"Jupier Hammond: America's First Afro-American Published Poet." http://lloydharborhistoricalsociety.org/jupiter.html.

Kiernan, Denise, and Joseph D'Agnese. *Signing Their Lives Away: The Fame and Misfortune of the Men Who Signed the Declaration of Independence*. Philadelphia: Quirk Books, 2009.

Kirby, David. "Nathan Hale Was Here...and Here...and Here." *New York Times*, November 23, 1997.

Kuehas, Thomas A. "Reluctant Host, Controlling Company: The Military Occupation of Rock Hall, 1776." *Nassau County Historical Society Journal* 47 (1992).

Ladd, Horatio Oliver. *The Origin and History of Grace Church, Jamaica, New York*. New York: Shakespeare Press, 1914. https://archive.org/details/originhistoryofg00/add.

Lengel, Edward G. *The Glorious Struggle: George Washington's Revolutionary War Letters*. New York: Harper Collins Publishers, 2007.

*Long Island Press*. "Jamaica: The Fight for Souls." June 27, 1976.

Luke, Myron, and Robert W. Venables. *Long Island in the American Revolution*. Albany: New York State American Revolution Bicentennial Commission, 1976.

Manley, Seon. *Long Island Discovery*. Garden City, NY: Doubleday & Company, Inc., 1966.

Mather, Frederic Gregory. *The Refugees of 1776 from Long Island to Connecticut*. Albany, NY: J.B. Lyon Company, Printers, 1913.

Maxwell, William G. *A Portrait of William Floyd, Long Islander*. Setauket, NY: Society for the Preservation of Long Island Antiquities, 1956.

*Meigs Battle of Sag Harbor*. Long Island Collection, East Hampton Library, DFA 233.

Metcalf, Reginald. *A Brief History of the Arsenal*. N.p.: Old Huntington Green, Inc., 1978.

Meyer, Lois J. *The Irony of Submission; The British Occupation and Long Island, 1776–1783*. Huntington, NY: Town Board, 1992.

Mollo, John, and Malcolm McGregor. *Uniforms of the American Revolution*. New York: MacMillan, 1975.

Moore, William H. *History of St. George's Church, Hempstead, Long Island, NY*. New York: E.P. Dutton, 1881. https://archive.org/details/historyofstgeorg00,moor.

Morris, Richard, ed. *Encyclopedia of American History*. New York: Harper & Row, 1965.

Muzzy, David Saville, PhD. *An American History*. New York: Ginn & Company, 1911.

Naylor, Natalie. *The Roots and Heritage of Hempstead Town*. Interlaken, NY: Heart of the Lakes Publishing, 1994.

Nell, William C. *The Colored Patriots of the American Revolution*. New York: Arno Press and the New York Times, 1968.

Norton, Mary Beth. *Liberty's Daughters: The Revolutionary Experience of American Women, 1750–1800*. Boston: Little, Brown and Company, 1980.

Onderdonk, Henry, Jr. *Documents and Letters Intended to Illustrate the Revolutionary Incidents of Queens County*. Port Washington, NY: Kennikat Press, 1970. Originally published, 1846.

————. *Revolutionary Incidents of Suffolk and Kings Counties: With an Account of the Battle of Long Island and the British Prisons and Prison-Ships at New York*. Port Washington, NY: Kennikat Press, 1970. Originally published, 1849.

O'Shea, John. *History of the Town of North Hempstead*. Manhasset, NY: Town Hall, n.d.

Overton, Jacqueline, ed. *Long Island's Story*. Garden City, NY: Doubleday & Company, 1932.

Pennypacker, Morton. *General Washington's Spies on Long Island and in New York*. Walnut Creed, CA: Aegean Park Press, n.d.

Pole, J.R., ed. *The Revolution in America, 1754–1788: Documents of the Internal Development of America in the Revolutionary Era*. Stanford, CA: Stanford University Press, 1970.

Quarles, Benjamin. *The Negro in the American Revolution*. Institute of Early American History and Culture, Williamsburg, VA. Chapel Hill: University of North Carolina Press, 1996.

*Queens Rangers 1ˢᵗ American Regiment*. Shelton, CT: Captain Robert McCrea's Company, n.d.

Radune, Richard. *Sound Rising: Long Island at the Forefront of America's Struggle for Independence*. Branford, CT: Research in Time Publications, 2011.

Reynolds, John. *Long Island: Behind the British Lines During the Revolution*. Setauket, NY: Society for the Preservation of Long Island Antiquities, 1960.

Riker, James, Jr. *The Annals of Newtown in Queens County, New York*. New York: D. Fanshaw, 1852.

Rines, Edward F. *Old Historic Churches of America*. New York: MacMillan Company, 1936.

Ross, Peter. *A History of Long Island from Its Earliest Settlement to the Present Time*. New York: Lewis Publishing Co., 1902. https://archive.org.details/historyoflongislross.

Schecter, Barnet. *The Battle for New York: The City at the Heart of the American Revolution*. New York: Walker & Company, 2002.

Schlesinger, Art. *The Colonial Merchants and the American Revolution*. New York: Athenaeum, 1968.

Schneider, Louis H. "British Occupancy of Flushing." *Long Island Forum* (December 1966).

Schultz, Bernice. *Colonial Hempstead*. Lynbrook, NY: Review-Star Press, 1937.

Seymour, George Dudley. *Documentary Life of Nathan Hale*. New Haven, CT: Tuttle, Morehouse & Taylor Company, 1941.

Smits, Edward. "Creating a New County: Nassau." In *The Long Island Historical Journal*, edited by Roger Wunderlich. Stony Brook, NY: Department of History, SUNY, 1999.

———. *The Creation of Nassau County*. Mineola, NY, 1960.

Spaulding, E. Wilder. *New York in the Critical Period*. New York: Columbia University Press, 1932.

Tallmadge, Benjamin. *Memoir of Col. Benjamin Tallmadge: Prepared by Himself at the Request of His Children*. New York: Thomas Holman, 1858.

Thompson, Benjamin F. *History of Long Island: From Its Discovery and Settlement to the Present Time*. 3rd ed. New York: Robert H. Dodd, 1918.

*A Toast to Freedom: New York Celebrates Evacuation Day*. New York: Fraunces Tavern Museum, 1984.

Van Santvoord, Peter Luyster. "Revolutionary Incidents of Oyster Bay Town." *Long Island Courant* 3, no. 1 (March 1967).

Vincitorio, Gaetano L. "The Revolutionary War and Its Aftermath in Suffolk County, Long Island." *Long Island Historical Journal* 7, no. 1 (September 1994).

Waller, Henry D. *History of the Town of Flushing.* Flushing, NY: J.H. Ridenour, 1899.

Wanzor, Leonard, Jr. *Patriots of the North Shore: Great Neck-Hempstead Harbor-Cedar Swamp-Wolver Hollow-Norwich-Oyster Bay-Jericho During the Revolutionary War.* Edited by Joshua Epstein. N.p., 1976.

Wettingfeld, Jan Brown. "Queens Tories Captured at Jamaica Hill." *Little Neck Ledger*, April 30, 1998.

Wilson, Rufus Rockwell. *Historic Long Island.* New York: Berkeley Press, 1902.

# Index

# About the Author

D r. Joanne Grasso is an Adjunct Assistant Professor of History and Political Science specializing as an "Americanist" in the areas of the American Revolution, the American presidency and the founding documents. She holds an interdisciplinary Doctor of Arts degree in Modern World History, two Master of Arts degrees in History and Government and Politics and a Bachelor of Arts degree in Politics, Economics and Society. Dr. Grasso is a member of the Daughters of the American Revolution (DAR), Society for Historians of the Early American Republic (SHEAR) and the American Revolution Round Table (ARRT) in New York City. Her past career was in the travel industry, and she has traveled extensively both internationally and throughout the United States, particularly to historic sites.

*Visit us at*
www.historypress.net
..............................................................
*This title is also available as an e-book*